I0199094

"Steve Bell works hard in this book to dispel stereotyping of ordinary Muslims. His concern is for ordinary Muslims whom ordinary Christians will meet at work or college or in local communities.

In a creative way, Steve helps Christians to interact in a confident yet humble manner with Muslim acquaintances and friends."

Rt. Rev. Dr Bill Musk, former bishop in Tunis

"This is one of the most important books that we must read in our present global crisis."

George Verwer

friendship
-FIRST-

Ordinary Christians
discussing good news
with ordinary Muslims

STEVE BELL

2016

INTERSERVE

Friendship First – the book (formerly Study Manual)

Copyright © Steve D. Bell
The right of Steve D. Bell to be identified as author of this work has been asserted by
him in accordance with the Copyright, Designs and patents Act 1988.

First published in 2003
Second edition 2009
Third edition 2011
Fourth edition 2016

No part of this publication may be reproduced or transmitted in any form or by any
means, electronic or mechanical, including photocopy, recording or any information
storage and retrieval system, without permission in writing from the publisher.

Unless otherwise indicated, biblical quotations are from the New Living Bible
Copyright © 1996 by Tyndale United Kingdom.

Unless otherwise indicated, all Qur'anic quotations are from A.Yusif Ali's
The Holy Qur'an - Text,Translation & Commentary.
Copyright © 1975 by The Islamic Foundation of Great Britain

British Library Cataloguing in Publication Data
A Catalogue record for this book is available from the British Library
ISBN 978-0-9957787-7-1

Produced by Interserve (Britain & Ireland), 5/6 Walker Avenue, Wolverton Mill, Milton
Keynes, MK12 5TW
Email: sales@kitab.org.uk
www.kitab.org.uk

Cover photo: © Pearl/Lightstock.com
Internal photos: Chapter 1 © Nazar Gonchar/Shutterstock.com, Chapter 2 © Frontiers
International & AWM International, Chapter 3 © Interserve, Chapter 4 © Steve Bell,
Chapter 5 © veneratio/Adobe Stock, Chapter 6 © Frontiers International, Chapter
7 © kamellita/Adobe Stock, Chapter 8 © oneinchpunch/Adobe Stock, Chapter 9 ©
Interserve, Chapter 10 © Frontiers International, Chapter 11 © Jasmin Merdan/Adobe
Stock, Chapter 12 © Pearl/Lightstock.com

Graphic design by Heather and Mark Knight
Logo design by Hugh Briscoe

Acknowledgements

I'm grateful to many friends who have influenced me in my pursuit of ways of embodying 'grace and truth' in gospel engagement with people from Muslim family backgrounds.

Name's which come to mind include in chronological order – Don Rowley; Monica & Jack Blockley (aka Abu and Oum Philippe); Bill Musk; Colin Chapman; Kenneth Bayley; Vivienne Stacey; Martin Goldsmith; Andrew Smith (alias "Smeee") and Bernie Power.

I'm also grateful for the patience of those who have been readers and checkers of the manuscript. These include Joseph Lee, Eddie Foulkes, Roxy, Dan Challis, Rachel Lee and Alan Howell.

Finally to Him for whom all this work has been done. May He take its content and so change the attitudes of 'ordinary' Christians that they will be compelled to develop friendly relationship with an 'ordinary' Muslim.

Steve Bell
October 2016

Contents

Introduction

When Christians think about "Islam" they tend to default to thinking only in technical terms about the religion. This tends to put many Christians off thinking any more about it. When Christians think about "Muslims" they tend to default to the negative media images which imply that all Muslims are both religious and violent. On both counts they are not.

The net result is a deeply suspicious and defensive 'us and them' attitude among many Christians. In fact one Christian leader said to me: 'Governments can't do anything so it's up to Christians to destroy Islam'. I struggle to align such opinions with the heart of Jesus who rebuked such attitudes saying: 'You don't know what kind of spirit you are of. (Lk.9:54-55). This is what drove me to write *Friendship First* – a book aimed at helping 'ordinary' Christians to discuss the good news about Jesus with 'ordinary' Muslims in an atmosphere of spiritual friendship rather than doctrinal combat. The place to start is to recognise the difference between "Islam" as a religion and a "Muslim" as a person.

I am using the word 'friendship' to refer to behaviours that earn us the right to be trusted by a Muslim who may then ask us for a reason why we are as we are. However, friendship is neither a quick-fix nor a 'silver-bullet'. It can be time consuming and requires commitment from us. This definition of friendship is not saying: 'I'm your friend so that you will follow Jesus; but 'I want you to follow Jesus because I'm your friend – and even if you don't follow Jesus, I'll still be your friend'.

Such friendships are no longer just for the so called full-time Christian 'specialists' but for ordinary Christians of all walks of life. Any Muslim who reads this book should not be unduly offended by anything in it. In fact it may even be useful if that Muslim is actively enquiring about Jesus; which is happening frequently these days.

Friendship First is not just a book to read straight through it's also intended to be a resource to retrieve information easily when the need arises due to a conversation with any Muslim you want to call a 'friend'.

This book will hopefully break down the traditional media stereotypes such as the idealised image of an old devout man with a long white beard telling his prayer beads and studying the Qur'an in an ornate atmosphere of a mosque; or the politicised image of a subservient woman wearing a face veil and keeping behind her husband. These images have some truth but not all the truth about the people we refer to as 'Muslim'. The reality is a mosaic or a spectrum of types.

In fact a significant proportion of Muslims are non-religious and many are secular. Many are young people or young professionals who have been raised in a twilight-zone between eastern and western culture.

I pray that this book will open your eyes; broaden your understanding and build-up your confidence to reach out to the people around you who are from a Muslim family background. Please join the thousands of Christians around the world who have read this book and gone on to participate in the accompanying small-group DVD / video course, which has caused them to adopt the life motto – "Friendship First".

CHAPTER ONE

Setting the Scene

True tolerance is to accept the other, not by ignoring the distance between us, but by measuring that distance accurately and by recognizing that whoever wants to cross over has the right and the freedom to do so. Only love can create the necessary conditions for the truth to emerge...

Chawkat Moucarry

If a Christian is being hostile or non-committal about Muslims I like to ask – not "What do you think about them?" but – "How do they make you feel?" Invariably their mental and emotional issue is rooted in four main issues – terrorism; migration; fear they will take over and a confusion between "Islam" as a religion and "Muslims" as people. So let's start with these issues.

Islamic violence has made many people (including Christians) afraid of Muslims. The word "Islamism" is now used to talk about "bad Muslims". Islamism is an ideology that has a political agenda. The aim is to force Islamic values on all spheres of life right across the globe and thereby usher in another golden-age of medieval Islam[1].

> *'Islamism' makes us afraid of Muslims but also helps us identify the 'bad' ones.*
>
> Steve Bell

They arrive at this aim because they have adopted a literal interpretation of the Qur'an, which they feel gives them permission to impose brutal sanctions on anyone who doesn't conform or who stands in their way – hence the burning of people in cages, beheading, crucifixions and the right to impose a form of sexual slavery on women.

At the core of this minority ideology is a mixture of 'demonic darkness' and 'corrupt human nature'. It is the most rudimentary and mediaeval form of Islam and demonstrates what it would look like if their ideology ever did prevail. That would be unthinkable as well as incompatible with international standards of human rights.

Islamism is like a parody of the Bible account where Joshua campaigned militarily to settle ancient Israel as a political nation-state under the rule of God. In the same way Islamist Muslims work towards *khalifa* which is their name for the rule of God on earth.

Let's be clear – this vision held by a minority of Muslims is back-firing. It's having the opposite effect as public opinion is shunning Islamists and Islam. Record numbers of Muslims are abandoning Islam saying: "If this is true Islam I don't want anything to do with it".

This rejection got under way when Islamist Muslims attacked America on 11 September 2001; an event referred to by the international intelligence community as a 'declaration of war on western values'; but it provoked the two Gulf Wars as western powers retaliated. Soon the so called 'Arab Spring' erupted as Muslim nations rose up to demand leadership that took them forwards rather than backwards. Islamist groups arose and names such as *ISIS, Al-Qaeda* and *Boko Haram* became household names.

The barbaric behaviour of these 'death-cults' helped create a tipping-point, which resulted in a flow of migration as people from Islamic lands fled their homes, creating the so called 'refugee highway' through Italy, Turkey and Greece and into 'culturally-Christian' Europe.

Things were further complicated as the mass exodus seemed to escalate the number of Islamist attacks across mainland Europe. Sadly they were carried out by people from migrant families who were either sympathetic to Islamist ideology or – even worse – Islamist infiltrators posing as refugees. Take for instance the attack in Paris on the satirical French magazine *Charlie Hebdo*; then several other shoot-outs on the streets of France and Belgium; a 17 year-old Afghan male used an axe on a train in south Germany; a 19 year-old Iranian male with mental health issues used a hand-gun in Munich; a Tunisian male with a mixture of mental health issues and ISIS sympathies used a lorry in Nice; then two 19 year-old North African males killed a Catholic priest in France before a Somali background male used a hand-gun on the streets of London.

On top of the Islamist issue, there is also an underlying suspicion by many that even in settled Muslim communities there are those who are biding their time and quietly using democracy to erode democratic freedoms and subvert the values of the host culture.

The reputation of Islam as a religious system is being seriously eroded and public opinion about Muslims has deteriorated in a climate of fear, resentment, polite racism and suspicion. This reminds me of Charles Dickens' opening line in his book *A Tale of Two Cities* where he says: 'It was the best of times it was the worst of times'. The same is true of the age we live in.

The current climate is in some ways 'the worst of times' for Christians to adopt a *friendship first* approach to people from a Muslim background. Yet it's also true to say that the 'worst of times' is actually creating the 'best of times' because followers of Jesus are now able to reach out to Muslims and get a better reception because the current turbulence is opening up the spiritual options for Muslims, including the possibility of finding a 'spiritual friend' who is a follower of Jesus; these two factors are contributing to the fact that more Muslims are changing allegiance to Jesus Christ today than at any other time in church history[2].

The behaviour of the minority, together with their online propaganda, gives the false impression that *all* Muslims are Islamist – they are not! But media coverage suggests to the world that Islam is waiting menacingly to brutalise non-Muslims and turn the world into a global Islamic state.

The 9/11 attacks on America were a turning-point because as a result:

- The world woke-up to the dark potential of politicised Islam (i.e. Islamism)

- Muslims worldwide were embarrassed and divided over Islamism

- Islam began to appear incompatible with the modern world

- Significant numbers of Muslims began to reassess their religious heritage.

An urban myth is that Islam is 'the fastest growing religion on earth'. But this is only due to a higher birth-rate in Islamic countries – not conversion. Without wishing to sound triumphalist or competitive, the statistics from the US Pew Research Center show that when it comes to 'conversion' growth Christians are the largest faith group (31% of the planet) and the conversion rate to Christ means Christianity is the fastest growing religion on earth[3]. So an Islamic take-over is highly unlikely either because the issue is less its growth and more about the defection going on as people leave Islam.

Yet many Christians are still convinced that Islam could become the religion of state in the democratic world. To my mind the points above show the idea is almost impossible for the following reasons:

Social & political reasons

- Islam could only take over in a European nation by the sovereign permission of God. Remember that in the Middle Ages political Islam was turned back by force of arms, at Paris and Vienna. Only his providence would permit Islam to take over in Britain or Europe now.[4]

- Speaking with the eye of faith, rather than Islam rising in the West, the opposite is more likely as its mediaeval expression drives public opinion against Islam. It could even prompt people to seek again the Judeo-Christian heritage and so cause a Christian 'spiritual awakening'.

- Only a small handful of Islamic states have ever managed to implement Islamic Law so it's a big stretch to imagine it could happen in a secular democracy.

- Far from an Islamic 'revival' the house of Islam is showing signs of being in a painful reform process as the internet helps younger Muslims to be aware of wider options.

Ideological reasons

- Islamist thinking is usually diametrically opposed to western values, which is why it sometimes violates internationally agreed standards of human rights.

- Islam has a 'deistic' (i.e. God-centred) worldview so the chances of it being adopted in any liberal democratic countries is about as remote as America adopting its arch-rival ideology – Communism.

- A British national census showed 5,000 white Britons had embraced Islam while 50,000 Anglo-Saxons are practising Buddhism, so which is the bigger 'threat'?

- Some Muslim leaders have gone on record about the economic failure in the Muslim World, which begs the question: 'Can Islam thrive in the modern world?' while the West and East Asia provide its technology and information.

It's clear that we need to keep the words "Islam" and "Muslim" in separate mental compartments and resist being unnecessarily suspicious of 'ordinary Muslims'; that is, until they give us reason to be so. In other words, why not give Muslims the benefit of the doubt?

STATISTICS

While most Muslims are peace-loving people, the following is true of political Islam. ...

- 90% of all refugees are from the Muslim World

- 90% of all conflicts are going on in the Muslim World

- Of the 25 countries where human rights violations are going on against non-conformists, 21 are Muslim states

Source: http://www.independent.co.uk/news/world/europe/refugee-crisis-six-charts-that-show-where-refugees-are-coming-from-where-they-are-going-and-how-they-10482415.html

In this 'worst' and 'best' of times Christians are in a strategic position because fair-minded Muslims see them as decent because they are 'People of the Book' the Bible (S3:64-71). This means Christians and Jews are not part of the 'house of Islam' (*dar ul-Islam*) but neither are they 'unbelievers' who belong to the 'house of war' (*dar al-Harb*). These phrases reflect the early frontier days of Islam when people were seen as either "in" or "out" (i.e. friend of foe).

Because Christians are neither friend nor foe they are well placed to walk out onto the bridge of friendship which can span the chasm between a Muslim's family background and the good news about Jesus.

At a time of history when the numbers of settled migrants are being added to by emergency migration, God's heart is that we should *'show love to the foreigners living among you'* (Deut.10:17) and also *'show hospitality to strangers'* (Heb.13:2). This book tries to explain how you can put this command into practice.

We feel deeply the humiliation, the marginalisation of the whole Muslim world. Muslim countries are so divided, so small, so irrelevant... We are the most backward among nations, and the poorest. Almost the whole of Islam belongs to the Third World. Part of the Middle East may have enormous oil resources, but, even there it is the West that ultimately controls them.

Dr Zaki Badawi, Chairman of the British Council of Mosques

Whatever the future holds the Bible urges us to adopt a 'grace and truth' response to everyone. And remember, Muslims had no choice about being born into the social and religious system they were. So no matter how negative the media images of Islamists get, God's "outrageous grace" is extended to all Muslim people. The same sovereign Lord who oversaw Islam's arrival on the world stage continues to guide history to his appointed end (Eph.1:11).

Christ, in his dealings with ordinary people around him, tended to free them from the 'ideal' religion of the professionals. Why educate the ordinary Muslims in their own faith so that Christ can meet them there tomorrow when he can meet them at the point of their felt-needs today?

Rt. Rev. Dr Bill Musk - former bishop in Tunis

New approaches to Muslims

The purely factual books about Islam have caused some Christians to either switch off or inadvertently start to talk to Muslims about Islam rather than Jesus. To complement the cerebral approach, *friendship first* enables you to relate to a Muslim as a human being in the round – their spirit, mind and circumstances. It's therefore a 'relational approach' similar to the way the apostle Paul related to individuals.

Take for instance his first letter to the Greek believers in Jesus at Corinth.

> *Our aim is that we relate to Muslims in such a way that the only offence we cause is that of the Cross.*
>
> Steve Bell

'I have become a slave to all people to bring many to Christ. When I was with the Jews, I lived like a Jew to bring the Jews to Christ. When I was with those who follow the Jewish law, I too lived under that law. Even though I am not subject to the law...When I am with the Gentiles who do not follow the Jewish law, I too live apart from that law so I can bring them to Christ...Yes, I try to find common ground with everyone, doing everything I can to save some.' (1 Cor.9:19-33).

Friendship First is also an 'apologetic approach' which means it commits to teasing out points that can help form a connection with a Muslim rather than pushing us further apart. This is a contrast with the opposite way, the *'polemic approach'* which assumes we are "poles apart" and can be combative, emphasising difference and contradictions between us that can generate more heat than light.

If we push people further away from Christ it is a weird sort of "un-evangelism", which seems to be an unworthy response to the Great Commission of Christ (Mat.28:18-20) where Jesus requires us to get alongside and 'disciple'. This means walking with people on their journey, hopefully to Christ, rather than away from him.

> *Often our first step is to recognise we have an attitude problem!*
>
> Steve Bell

So I hope this book won't merely 'inform' you but also 'affect' you. It's not just another A,B,C about Islam but an A, E, I, O, U of Christian friendship with a Muslim. It aims to affect your...

A - attitude

Pause now and reflect on your attitude to Muslims. We need to foster a Christly attitude to 'the stranger in the midst'. Human nature is race-conscious, which can lead to over-compensation (i.e. polite forms of racism). The British Commission for Racial Equality did some important work during a period when "institutional racism" was discovered in public life, including the police and armed forces.

Having said that people can also have genuine concerns about the social issues surrounding increased migration which could strain national amenities. The British 'Brexit' vote to leave the European Union prompted widespread racial abuse in the UK, possibly by those of the political 'right wing' who felt emboldened by the national mood.

What we do know is that it is a counter-cultural social statement when a Christian adopts a welcoming attitude towards an immigrant.

E - emotions

Pause again and reflect on how Muslims make you "feel". We need to deal with our negative emotions, particularly fear or resentment of the presence of 'foreigners'. The Bible says *'the earth is the Lord's and everything in it...'* (Ps.24:1) yet some Christians actually resent the Muslim presence in, what they refer to as, "our" country. An important step towards genuine friendship with a Muslim person is to recognise where we have such assumptions lurking in our own subconscious mind, causing negative feelings towards the perceived 'outsider'.

Emotions are often stirred up when we compare the best of our own culture with the worst of Muslim culture; for example holding the view that Muslim culture is somehow inferior to our own way of life. But there are aspects of Muslim culture that are actually more biblical and therefore potentially more "civilised" than the western morality of convenience. One example is the value placed on old age and how the elderly are cared for. There are no homes for the elderly in the Muslim world where ageing members of the extended family (not just parents) are included within the home. The aim in this book is to help you discover how to become more open to God's heart and mind on such issues.

I - information

We need to understand what makes Muslims tick but the information needs to be balanced and accurate. So when we have faced our hidden attitude and emotions towards Muslim people, we are in a better position to receive balanced information.

For example, because Islam is seen by some scholars as an 'Arabised reflection of Judaism', a Muslim may well carry in their mind, enough background knowledge (however sketchy and inaccurate) which has the potential to sensitise them to the gospel when they hear it explained appropriately.

We will see in chapter 3 that Muslims have already grasped some important foundational ideas – i.e. about God; Jesus; the 'Spirit of God';

submission to God's will; prayer; fasting; godly living; heaven; hell; and a judgement day. So they can be helped to find completion of what they know, in Christ.

O - opportunities

With our attitude and emotions aligned, and receiving more balanced information, we can take advantage of the increasing God-given opportunities to interface with people from a Muslim background. Such opportunities are coming our way much more these days. Ordinary Muslims need to meet God-fearing followers of Jesus who they can trust. For this to happen, ordinary Muslims need ordinary Christians to get alongside them.

Mission is now from everywhere to everywhere; the world is living in our postcode.

Steve Bell

The Bible is clear that it's God who oversees the movements of people in human history (Acts 17:26-27). We can therefore assume that the migration patterns of peoples around the planet come within the scope of divine sovereignty. So one outcome of Muslim migration to the West is that they are finding faith in Jesus. If they are seizing the opportunity, are we? Now pause again to assess what opportunities and points of contact exist around you.

The church has been unsuccessful in bringing Muslims to Christ for hundreds of years. We have tried to evangelise them, found it hard and labelled them difficult and resistant, rather than questioning our Western presumptions about how to communicate the gospel effectively to them in terms they can understand.

Giulio Basetti-Sani

U - understanding

The result of all of the above is that we gain some understanding of people from a Muslim background that can develop to the extent that we can become effective witnesses to the grace of God in Jesus Christ.

Wrong ideas about Islam

Although – in one sense – we can't separate a Muslim (the person) from Islam (her religion), nevertheless in another sense we can and must. It's possible because a Muslim as an individual is just one unit in a system that is predominantly cultural rather than religious. The religious aspect, however critical and non-negotiable, is often window-dressing to the deeper psyche of a Muslim who may not actually be practising at all. This is why each Muslim's experience, understanding of and adherence to Islam varies from one to another. If you're not from a Muslim family it's hard to grasp this. But rather than becoming frozen to the spot let's start taking the available opportunities among Muslims that are presenting themselves. Some Christians shrink back due to a number of issues:

- Some suffer because their head and heart is negatively affected by the stereotypes of the media and Christian pulp-fiction, which usually focusses on the worst behaviour of the minority, while ignoring the majority.

- Some feel overwhelmed and so give way to a sense of defeat before they start.

- Some retreat to become 'armchair critics' of both Muslims and the Christians who are doing something positive to relate to them.

- Some convince themselves Muslims should be left to so called "specialists".

- Some feel all Muslims are religious and believe the same thing. According to a British census only about 40% of British "Muslim men" are in mosque on a Friday. Many are as "Muslim" as an Anglo-Saxon is "Church of England".

'I knew a Muslim family which, due to a tragedy, had left their homeland. One evening my wife and I visited them. After fun-filled interaction with the children, I asked how they were enjoying my home country. We found they had been in the country a year but had never seen the inside of a home. They were lonely and eager for friendship. The sad thing was there were Bible-believing churches close by. Not one church member had called on this family'.

Wrong attitudes to Muslims

A man once asked me: "Would you give me some hints on how to give the gospel to a Muslim at work"?. He was visibly surprised to get the answer "No". He retorted "But aren't you an expert on this?" Eventually we struck a deal that when he was able to view that Muslim as a *friend* (rather than a post-box to drop the gospel into like a letter) then I could help him. He did get it, and started to see that he needed to *relate* to the Muslim people around him rather than merely *confronting* them. The gospel is best shared, not in confrontation but 'spiritual friendship'.

Become a real friend to a Muslim!

Steve Bell

Friendship is about the normal stuff of everyday life – such as doing a favour for each other; having a meal or drinking tea together; talking about the things that matter to you; giving gifts to one another; listening and being prepared to be vulnerable, laughing and simply enjoying one another's company.

Spiritual hunger leads them

Someone who had participated in a *Friendship First* Course told me: "Friendship isn't a short-cut, but it is a smoother road-surface to travel on with someone".

It's now clear from research that the spiritually thirsty Muslim, like anyone else, is drawn to the person of Jesus Christ as a result of what boils down to a mixture of 'heart-hunger' and intellectual curiosity. A Muslim person should not be thought of as merely having wrong doctrine that needs correcting. Remember that Islam (and the Qur'an) like Judaism (and the Bible) are both culturally Semitic. Both books carry a mind-set and assumptions which (at least in part) resonate with each other[5].

In fact Islam has an advantage over Christian heresies such as the Jehovah's Witness movement, in that Islam is – partially at least – a more biblical worldview; in fact it can even be ahead of secular humanism in this respect.

As a religious ideology Islam attempts to lead Muslims to the "Islamic wellhead"; however, like the well in Sychar (Jn.4) the Islamic well is also deep and there is no bucket to draw with. Even when the scent of 'living' water can be detected from the biblical influence in Islamic tradition, it seems marred by the 'traditions of men' which have developed over the centuries within Islam. This denies Muslims the spiritual drink, from Jesus Christ, they are lacking.

Like the Apostle Paul in his letter to the Roman church, I have sensed many Muslims sighing inwardly out of spiritual weariness that has come about from trying to live out religious regulations in their own strength. As Paul put it in Judaism, *'Oh what a miserable person I am! Who will free me from this life that is dominated by sin?'* (Rom. 7:24).

A potential open door is that Muslims are encouraged by the Qur'an, to relate in 'the best possible way' (S29.46; 3.64) to Jews and Christians (i.e. People of the Book). Through friendship with a Muslim we can steer away from the common point-scoring that goes on from both sides and relationship which enables a Muslim friend to begin from where he or she is and to explore the signposts to Christ which exist in Bible and even within the Qur'an itself[6].

Sources:

1 A definition of 'Islamism' - https://en.wikipedia.org/wiki/Islamism
2 David Garrison, *A Wind in the House of Islam*, 2014
3 Pew Research Center, April 23, 2015
   http://www.pewresearch.org/fact-tank/2015/04/23/why-muslimsare-the-worlds-fastest-growing-religious-group/)
4 Philip Jenkins, *God's Continent – Christianity, Islam and Europe's religious Crisis*, Oxford University Press, 2009
5 Ida Glasser, *Thinking biblically about Islam* Langham Global Press, 2016
6 The Camel Method,

CHAPTER TWO

What is a Muslim?

Modern Islamism is weak and brittle – not strong; which accounts for its shrillness. It will be dangerous for some time to come and its withdrawing roar may be long and bloody – but withdraw it will. The fanatics don't represent a resurgence of Islam but its death rattle.

William Theodore Dalrymple,
When Islam breaks down

The mental image of a Muslim – at least in popular perception – is either a stereotype such as a woman hidden behind a face-veil; or else a wild-eyed fanatic. Sometimes the stereotypes are benign, such as the idealised image of a wise old man with a long beard sitting cross-legged on a carpeted mosque floor studying an open Qur'an on a book stand while clutching prayer beads.

Such images – positive and negative – can be misleading because the different groups within Islam are a spectrum. Each Muslim community around the world is starkly different from others; no two seem alike. Each individual Muslim is also different because they are human beings and not soldier ants.

Generational differences

Today a large proportion of Muslims are under 25 years of age. On the outside they can appear to be well integrated into their host society and able to accommodate secular values. But for the younger generations of Muslims, social media has provided a safe-space to question Islam and the 'honour and shame' code. This often results in a greater openness to issues such as the freedom of religion and the role of women.

The two extremes of the wise devout and the young trendy Muslim are a stark reminder of the contrast between the older and younger generations. Muslim leaders have told me how they are struggling to broker the tension between the generations and how they feel they are losing their young people to secular pressures.

Differences in the practise of Islam

Having outlined these generational differences there is also a wide spectrum of difference. For example, there are 'non-religious' Muslims; there are those who are devout (young and old); there are so called 'moderate' Muslims who are middle-of-the-road or can even be more 'liberal'; there are 'nominal' or non-practising Muslims and – like Evangelical Christians – there are 'conservatives' and even charismatic types among the *Suffi* Muslims.

However, a problem is posed by the radical Islamist types who are hard liners. So it's virtually impossible to write anything about Muslims that will equally apply to all of these categories.

Most Muslims fall into the following categories	
non-religious	non-practising, Islam is their conscience
open	other religions are fine, all religion pleases God
moderate	Islam is best but others are tolerated
traditional	nominal and uninformed
conservative	Islam is the best religion
radical	Islam is the only valid religion
Islamist	Islam must be implemented globally at all costs

Broad guidelines about Muslim identity

Whatever comes into our heads when we think of the word "Muslim" will help us engage with our personal thoughts, attitude and feelings about them. It will also influence what sort of information about them we are prepared to entertain, as well as the kind of opportunities we're likely to grasp in order to meet them. It all depends on our previous experience of them - or lack of it.

In short, our attitude can be broadly described as "positive", "negative" or "indifferent". Which one do you think is you? Perhaps like many others, you find your attitude is a mixture of all three and maybe more. How do the following groups make you feel?

Negative stereotypes of Islam

- ISIS
- Al-Qaida
- Palestinian violent activists
- The Taliban
- The Gulf Wars
- Saddam Hussein
- Oil riches controlled by ruling families while the masses are poor
- Mass prayer line-ups, such as on Hajj
- Totalitarian regimes such as Yemen or Syria
- Women in 'purdah' (see glossary)

We now know that although some of the above involve individual Muslims, it is still true to say that a "Muslim" is not the same thing as "Islam" – in the same way that a Cuban is not "Communism". This becomes obvious when we meet a Muslim asylum-seeker who has suffered at the hands of an Islamic political regime. Here are some positive stereotypes of Muslim people.

Most asylum-seekers are fleeing Islamic lands; imagine how they feel when the ideology of their birth turns against them.

Steve Bell

Positive stereotypes of Muslims
- Commitment to family values & responsibilities
- Respect for the elderly
- Morally based & God-centred
- Sincerity in religious practice, even when poor
- Modesty of dress
- Beautiful architecture
- Saintly old Muslim scholars
- Tolerant Muslim spokespersons
- Suffering victims from Iraq and Syria
- Beautiful Arabic calligraphy

A letter from a radical Muslim thanked social activist Mary Whitehouse CBE for her Christian stand for moral standards on TV - *New Christian Herald 18 May 2002*

'As a Muslim I was inspired and moved by Mary's holy campaign to protect our society. Her campaign is an Islamic campaign and our duty as Muslims is to support her. I believe our Muslim leaders have neglected the damage caused by our immoral media and sexually sick and obsessed society.

I wanted to say to Mary before she died: "Thank you for what you have done and for alerting Muslims to this danger; thank you for giving us the hope that we can make a change in society".'

Dr A Majid Katme (Islamic Concern, Palmers Green, London)

The Bible compels us to relate to strangers

(Acknowledgement - Colin Chapman 'You go and do the same')

So whether they are "good", "bad" or "ugly"; God loves Muslims. Have a read of the following biblical verses and see how you would answer these questions.

Exodus 22:21; 23:9	
Leviticus 19:33-34	
Deuteronomy 10:17-20	What are the implications of these verses for Christians in a society that is receiving Muslim migrants today? What must it feel like to be an immigrant?
Matthew 5:43-48	'Love your neighbour' means those beyond your own community. How do you feel about that?
Matthew 7:12	How would you like your Muslim neighbour to treat you/your community? How does this affect the way you treat them?
Acts 9:10-19	What lay behind Ananias' doubts and suspicions? Where does 'saving face' come into the story?
Acts 10:1-48	What was Peter's mental blockage about Gentiles? Do you have a similar prejudice?
Galatians 1:21-24	Do you struggle to believe that Muslims can change allegiance to Jesus – if so why? If not, why not?
1 Timothy 2:1-6	How far can Paul's description of Jewish devotion be applied to Muslims?

Thinking 'Christianly' about Muslims

We have established that Muslims are first and foremost, human beings for whom Christ died. So our thinking needs to be based on God's view of humankind as described in the Bible, which teaches:

1 Human nature is not totally corrupt however, all of our nature is affected by the corruption of sin in every area of life. Even our worship of God will be tainted, according to Paul's observation: *'Nothing good lives in me'* (Rom.7:18).

2 A remnant of God remains in all humankind, including Muslims. If the word "godless" can be applied to many western societies, it isn't true of Muslim societies. For this reason, most Muslims are aware of the Islamic teaching about Jesus; sadly though in Islamic texts, he's a figure that bears little resemblance to the New Testament person. They are so near yet so far from the biblical revelation of the authentic Jesus.

If we scratch where Muslims are not itching we will only irritate them.

Steve Bell

Ethnic and cultural diversity of Muslims

A Muslim is not a Muslim is not a Muslim. This is because they are from various racial groupings. Muslims therefore have needs, which are specific to their own ethnic group. Whether born in an adoptive country or not, a Muslim can appear to indigenous people to be a 'stranger in the midst'. But they are not alone because so was Joseph in Egypt (Gen.37:12-36; 39-50), and Ruth in Israel (Book of Ruth), the Israelis in Exile (see Psalm 137) and Paul and his companions in their apostolic travels (Acts 13-14, 16-20, 28:1-10). Here are some of the many ways in which Muslims differ from each other:

Status
- Refugees
- Asylum seekers
- Economic migrants
- Foreign students
- Resident immigrants
- Westernised 2nd or 3rd generation immigrants

Race
- Indo-Pakistan sub-continent - Indian, Pakistani, Bangladeshi
- Middle East - Egyptian, Palestinian, Kurdish, Iranian, Iraqi, Jordanian
- Gulf - Yemeni

- North Africa - Moroccan, Algerian, Tunisian
- Africa - Somali, Nigerian
- Europe – Albanian, Bosnian, Turkish
- South East Asia - Malaysian, Filipino, Singaporean

The question is: how can we develop a Christly attitude to such diversity of race, nationality and culture? The Bible says:

'Do not take advantage of foreigners who live among you in your land. Treat them like native-born Israelites, and love them as you love yourself.' (Lev.19:33-34)

'...I was a stranger and you invited me into your home...' (Mt.25:35) (NLT)

Language
Muslims speak many languages that can be quite foreign to one another.
- Asians may speak Baluchi, English, Dari, Farsi, Gujerati, Pashtu, Silleti, Urdu
- Middle Easterners speak Arabic (various dialects), Kurdish (various dialects)
- Europeans may speak Albanian, Russian, Serbian, Turkish
- Africans may speak Bantu, English, French, Hausa, Somali, Swahili

Western-born Muslims
Muslims who were born in the West and are under 30 years of age tend to be more culturally assimilated and some will hold to Islam more lightly – if at all, to the sadness of their parents.

The non-religious in this age-range are able to relate to contemporary youth and student culture and are 'digital natives'. Having said this, the challenge of radicalisation is real and recruiters prey on this generation, particularly those that have failed in the education system and may be unemployed, or those engaged in criminal behaviour and are serving prison time. It's those who feel marginalised that are more prone to listen to extremist propaganda on social media. Such young Muslims can find in Islam, a racial and cultural identity and/or a coping mechanism in what can be a hostile or even Islamophobic society that merely "tolerates" them.

On the other hand, middle-aged and elderly Muslims tend to genuinely adhere to Islam as part of their more traditional outlook on life and a moral compass in what they perceive to be a 'godless' host society.

An outsider looking in at this issue might comment that Christians and Muslims have more in common than meets the eye; and that as people from faith communities in a secular world, if they would only stop stereotyping each other and start relating to each other as people, they might just get a pleasant surprise at what they find.

CHAPTER THREE

The Basic Teaching of Islam

Whatever is just and good in other religions finds its deepest meaning and its final perfection in Christ.

Giulio Bassetti Sani

Islam was founded in Saudi Arabia by a merchant called Muhammad al-Quraishi (570-632 AD). It's a religion based on a book - the Qur'an, which Muslims believe was dictated verbatim over a period of 23 years to Muhammad, who is thought to have been illiterate (S7.158). The Qur'an says that its message originated from an 'Eternal Tablet' in heaven (S6.92; 43:3-4) and is to be accepted without question. The text is thought to have been dictated by the Angel Gabriel (S2.97), also by other angels (S15.8), as well as by the Holy Spirit (S26.192-194). It also claims direct divine inspiration (S53.2-18).

The process of getting the dictated 'revelation' into written form involved Muhammad remembering what he believed he had heard from God. At a later time, Muhammad would recite the material to scribes who wrote it down on anything that came to hand. Several years later the fragments were collected and assembled; but critics say there was interference from the people who collated the fragments to assemble the material. This is difficult to verify either way because this sort of rigorous academic scrutiny of the Qur'an is forbidden, on the grounds that it would be blasphemous.

THINK OF IT LIKE THIS...

The Qur'an teaches the existence of the Eternal Tablet, which has always existed in heaven. This seems to contradict the Islamic teaching that nothing lives with God in heaven - no son - nothing! Yet the Eternal Tablet is a direct parallel of the New Testament verse: 'In the beginning the Word already existed. He was with God and He was God... So the Word became flesh and made his home among us...' (Jn.1:1-2,14). Jesus is the Eternal Tablet that was with God and came amongst men.

The Qur'an's 114 chapters (*suras*) are written in classical Arabic. This is a high form that is to Arabic what the language of William Shakespeare is to English. Although Christians don't accept it to be "inspired" in the biblical sense, it seems only fair to say that the Qur'an is no less inspired than the beauty of Shakespeare. In spite of its grammatical errors its linguistic beauty and power impact Arabic speakers; though many less educated Muslims understand little of its classical language. Almost the length of the New Testament, each chapter (*sura*) is arranged in order of length from the longest to the shortest. It's not chronological which can be confusing. The Qur'an was received in two cities – Mecca, the birthplace of Muhammad and Medina where he fled under persecution.

Meccan Suras (611-622 AD)

The Meccan suras were received when Muslims were in the minority. On the whole, they are more diplomatic and spiritual and deal with issues similar to those of the minor prophets of the Old Testament; for example the call to worship one God; righteous living and social justice, such as caring for the poor and vulnerable.

Medinan Suras (623-632 AD)

The Medinan suras emerged when Muhammad was being resisted, though the Muslims were becoming the majority influence along the western coastal region of Saudi Arabia at that time. These suras are more assertive, intolerant and even condoning violence, which reflects the process that was going on where the Islamic tradition was blending the earthly and the spiritual. This is why Islam is a political religion and we see Islamists trying to bring back a literal implementation of this.

The basic teaching of Islam is comparatively simple. The language used to express it is Arabic, which is a 'root' language. This means that words are built up on a root structure. For example **s-l-m** is the root for the word Islam which means submission (i.e. to God).

A *Muslim* (male) or a *Muslima* (female) is someone who submits to God. The same root also gives us the word **salam** (peace through submission to God).

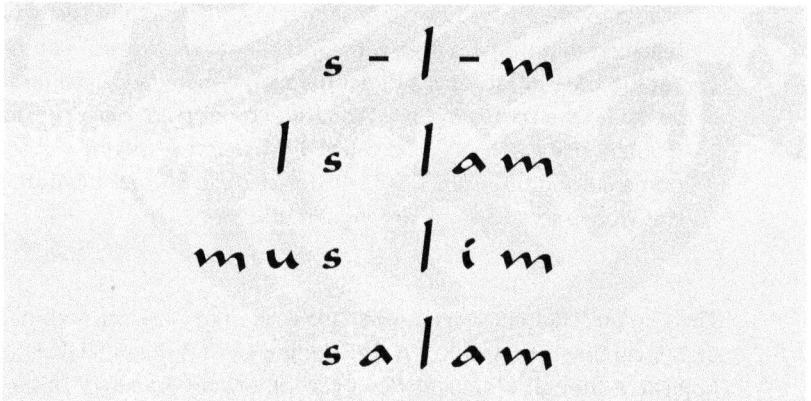

$$s - l - m$$

$$l \; s \quad l \; a \, m$$

$$m \, u \; s \quad l \; i \, m$$

$$s \, a \, l \, a \, m$$

The Five Pillars (*Arkan al-Islam*) - The Muslim's practical duty (*din*)

1 Declaration of Faith (*shahada*)

The word "*shahada*" is an Arabic word meaning "certification", "testimony" or "witness". So a *shahid* is a witness, and is used to describe Muslim martyrs such as suicide bombers. The *shahada* is the basic confession of

Islam, which is "There is no god but Allah and Muhammad is His apostle".

2 Prayer (salat)

Islam prescribes that a Muslim should pray five times a day as follows:

- *fajr* - dawn
- *zuhr* - mid-day
- *asr* - mid-afternoon
- *maghreb* - sunset
- *isha* - nightfall

3 Alms giving (zakat, S2.271-273)

The prescribed alms to be given is 2.5% of the money left after routine bills are paid.

Zakat is usually given for the maintenance of the local mosque and direct to the poor in the community.

4 Fasting (sawm, S2.183-187)

There are various annual fasts but Ramadan is the most well-known and, and it's the longest i.e. a lunar month. A Muslim fast is from food, liquid, cigarettes and sexual intercourse between the hours of sunrise and sunset. The fasting Muslim will also try not to experience anything that might tempt their imagination, so if they indulge in a wrong thing they count their fast as broken.

It's possible for Muslims to exempt themselves from fasting if they are a child; sick; travelling; pregnant or a nursing mother. Doctors often treat more people for stomach complaints due to over eating during periods of fasting than at any other time of the year. This is because after sunset, Islamic fasts are 'feasts' in the biblical sense.

5 Pilgrimage (Hajj, S2.196-197)

All Muslims who are able-bodied are expected to make a pilgrimage to Mecca at least once in a lifetime. Pilgrims visit Mecca and Medina, the twin holy cities associated with Muhammad's life. In Mecca they walk around the *ka'aba*. This is the edifice draped in black silk with Qur'anic verses embroidered on it.

Many Muslims believe that all personal sin is forgiven on *hajj* and so Muslims will often wait until later on in their lives to make this expensive journey. However the event is far from safe as statistics show (see page 38)

6 Struggle in the way of Islam (jihad)

This is not strictly a pillar of Islam. However, it is the principle underlying all the pillars and so is *de facto* the sixth pillar. The word *jihad* is an Arabic word, related to 'struggle' or 'strive'.

Every effort should be made by a Muslim to 'struggle' in the way of Islam by performing the five pillars and to take on their own human imperfections in a parallel to the apostle Paul's teaching on *'striving to keep your body under subjection'* in order to serve Christ (1 Cor.9:24-27AV). *Jihad* can also be expressed in violent resistance where Islamic interests are being threatened or damaged. However, Muslims disagree strongly with one another over, what many see, as the unwarranted abuse of the concept by Islamists who use it as a way of condoning their violent agenda towards non-Muslims as a political act of Islamic expansion.

STATISTICS

Death on the *Hajj*

1979   153 killed and 560 injured in a hostage incident

1987   400 Iranians died in clashes with police

1988   1 died and 16 injured in a bombing thought to be linked to Al-Qaeda

1990   1,426 died of suffocated in a tunnel caused by a fire in Medina

1991   200 Egyptians drowned enroute to Mecca when a ferry sank

1994   270 killed in a stampede in Mecca

1997   217 killed and 1,290 injured in a fire

1998   118 trampled to death and 180 injured

2001   35 trampled to death in a stampede

2003   14 trampled to death in a stampede

2004   251 killed and another 244 injured in a stampede

2006   346 killed and 289 injured in a stampede

2015   2,236 killed in a stampede

Source: https://www.theguardian.com/world/2006/jan/13/saudiarabia

The six beliefs of Islam (Al-Iman) - The Muslim's faith (iman)

1 Allah (tawhid, S37.35)
Muslims believe that God is one. The Arabic word *tawhid* literally means 'oneness' or 'unity' of God. Traditionally there are many names for God and Muslims relish the
ninety-nine 'Most Beautiful Names', which are attributed to Him. The Qur'an is clearer about what He is *not* rather than what He is. (S112.1-4)

2 The Angels (mala'ikatuhu, S35.1)
An important part of the biblical content of Islam is the belief in angels; four of them archangels, including Gabriel and an infinite number of 'ordinary' angels. Muslims also believe in beings which are somewhere between the angels and humankind. These are called *jinn*. Some of these are thought to be good, some evil and some neutral. In the magical expressions of Islam (i.e. "folk Islam") the *jinn* are placated and their help sought.

3 The Books (kutubuhu, S2.177)
Although Islam is a religion of 'the book' – the Qur'an, it's also a religion of several other lesser books which are referred to as 'The Books' as follows:

- The Scrolls of Abraham (now lost)
- Tawrat by Moses - **Torah** i.e. first five books of the Bible
- Zabur by David - **Psalms** and the Wisdom Literature
- Injil by Jesus - **Gospel**
- Qur'an by Muhammad - **Qur'an**
- Hadith - **Traditions** i.e. included but not strictly one of 'the books'

Islam venerates all these books, which provides an open door to encourage a Muslim to read the Bible for themselves. All books that came prior to the Qur'an are understood to be subsumed and superseded by the Qur'an. The books are also believed to have originated in heaven as the 'Eternal Tablet' and from there they were 'sent down' (*tanzil*) to mankind through different prophets at key points throughout history.

4 Prophetic Messengers (nabiim, S35.24)
Some Muslims believe there have been as many as 124,000 prophets. The Qur'an names about 25, and 21 of these are found in the Bible; for example Adam; Noah; Abraham; Moses; Elijah; Job; and John Baptist. The top five 'messengers' of Islam are generally agreed as follows…

- Adam - **Adam** the first man
- Ibrahim - **Abraham** the first Muslim and the father of faith
- Musa - **Moses** the law-giver
- Isa - **Jesus** the Word of God
- Muhammad - **Muhammad** the last & greatest prophet

5 The Judgement (*yawm uddin* S2.62)

This is the great day of recompense when good and bad deeds will be weighed in the divine balance and the fate of every soul decreed. All people will be assigned either to Paradise or to Hell at the discretion of God. Some Muslims also believe in a kind of purgatory, which is not actually taught in the Qur'an.

6 Allah's Decrees (*al-Qadr*)

God predestines everything both good and evil. Fatalism is therefore strong within the minds of Muslims who often hold to the mental picture of God as being capricious and unpredictable. Like the Christian understanding, orthodox Islamic teaching tries to hold a balance between the action of God and human responsibility.

The Call to Prayer (*athaan*)

The following words are intoned by the one who calls Muslims to prayer from the minaret of the mosque – *the muezzin*.

God is most great. I bear witness that there is no god except God.
I bear witness that Muhammed is the apostle of God.
Come to prayer.
Come to good.
Prayer is a better thing than sleep.
Come to the best deed.
God is most great. God is most great.
There is no god but God.

The first sura of the Qur'an *(fatiha)*

The Arabic word fatiha means 'opening' or 'beginning'. It comes from the same word that's used in the title Al-Fatah, the well-known Palestinian resistance Group. The following words are used in the opening sura of the Qur'an. Notice that it doesn't contain anything an evangelical Christian would fundamentally disagree with.

In the Name of the merciful Lord of mercy.
Praise be to God, the Lord of all being,
The merciful Lord of mercy,
Master of the Day of Judgement.
Thee alone we worship
And to Thee alone we come for aid.
Guide us in the straight path,
The path of those whom Thou hast blessed,
Not of those against whom there is displeasure,
Nor of those who go astray.

Translation - Kenneth Cragg - The Event of the Qur'an pg74

CHAPTER FOUR

Why do Muslims Follow Islam?

Among the factors contributing to the rise of Islam was the failure of institutional Christianity in love, in purity, in fervour and in spirit. Islam therefore developed in an environment of imperfect Christianity… This is the tragedy of the rise of Islam, which claims to displace what it has never really known

Bishop Kenneth Cragg

There are 1.6 billion Muslims in the world according to the estimate of the Pew Research Center (2010). This is roughly 23% of the global population. The sovereignty of God means that the birth and growth of Islam cannot be a mistake but something he is using for his own purpose – not least enabling Muslims to have some background ingredients of the gospel, which can be helpful when they encounter it. God 'works out everything in conformity with the purpose of his will.' (Eph.1:11)

There are several reasons why Muslims follow Islam. Here are some of them ...

1 Muslims are born into Islam

Unlike the West, personal identity comes through being born Muslim. In a God-centred culture this is such a central feature that it can be more important than nationality. A Muslim also expects that a non-Muslim who is born in Europe is a 'Christian'. So to the Muslim mind Hitler was "a Christian".

2 Islam is also a 'culture'

Islamic culture underlies every level of the Muslim's social network including the immediate family, the extended family and the wider clan. Islam is so intertwined with society that it rarely occurs to a Muslim to question this close-knit relational system. It is important to realise that Muslim culture is related to the biblical social-structure, which provides stronger cohesion than that of the West.

3 Many Muslims are nominal

A significant number of Muslims, particularly younger ones find themselves born into Muslim families but they are neither convinced nor formally practicing Islam – many are even nominal and fairly secular. For example a Turkish student said to me: "I'm not *mu'min*" (a true believer). There are many Muslims out there who pay lip-service to religious Islam but are, sometimes, very westernised in their lifestyle and interpretation of Islamic culture.

4 For some, Islam is a haven in a world of moral choices

The positive side to Islamic dogma is that Islam does give clear moral guidelines. The Muslim is instructed what to think and do from the moment they get out of bed to the moment they go to bed, and even what goes on while they are there. Some Muslims are clearly clinging tightly to Islam out of rejection of Western moral and spiritual values (or

It is in the theology of history ... that the deep causes of (Islam) must be sought.

Msgr. Paul Mary Mulla

lack of them) as well as materialism. Some western converts to Islam are the type, who prefer to have life's decisions simplified and choices minimised for them.

The appeal of Islam

Islam carries a natural appeal to a variety of people for a number of reasons depending on where in the world they are.

In the developing world

- The appeal to some African societies, which practice 'traditional religion' is that Islam is the newest of the world religions. This causes Muslims to assume Islam is in some sense more up-to-date than the others.

- To non-Westerners Islam appears to be culturally indigenous. This means it seems to be separated from anything Western in origin - unlike Christianity, which tends to be seen as a product of (if not a political tool of) the West.

- The non-Western persona of Islam is attractive in the post-colonial era. Of course in reality, Islam was born in the same part of the world as Christianity and therefore into a similar culture. Many Muslims were involved in the slave trade through the colonial period. In fact the word 'Abd in Arabic has roots which mean both "black" and "slave", which were synonymous. It's believed that girls from Asia and Africa are still being taken as "servants" to Gulf destinations today.[1]

- The apparent worldwide brotherhood (Umma) of Muslims is attractive in poorer countries. In reality there is a racial hierarchy amongst Muslims with the Arabs being the first class Muslims and Africa and Asia or the Far East as second and third class Muslims.

In the West

Western converts are more often from the black communities of America and the UK. These believers have suffered from racial discrimination and the lowest socio-economic conditions in crime-ridden areas. Today there are increasing numbers of Christian families who have a family member or friend who has converted to Islam. The following are the top three reasons given to Jay Smith during research amongst American converts to Islam.

1 Firstly Islam's social laws and the promise of order and stability is the most common reason for conversion. Islam is perceived to have the clout to deal with crime and injustices in society.

2 Secondly, the unity of God (*Tawhid*) is the next common reason. Islam offers a simple approach with no Trinity or intercessory mediator like Jesus. The Muslim is responsible for his or her own 'salvation'.

3 Thirdly the notion of the brotherhood of Islam was next. Islam endows the convert with a sense of the identity of God himself and the might of Islam as a body of people. This is particularly attractive to the marginalised.

Another reason why westerners convert to Islam includes the simplicity of Islam's teaching. The things a Muslim is required to believe are simple and the practice of them is comparatively easy. Unlike Christianity, Islamic dogma is quantifiable so the Muslim knows how they are doing. The tenets are to be accepted as written, without any interpretation or criticism. They are easily grasped and are palatable to the human mind. Islam does not require the revelation of the Holy Spirit to understand it, nor repentance nor a 'new birth' in order to live it.

Some Muslims will argue that the requirements of Islam are more reasonable and achievable (e.g. polygamy and easy divorce). For such Muslims, Islam is less hypocritical than Christianity, which attempts what they see as the impossible. Some Muslims also see Christianity as being professed in theory but abandoned in practice in the post-Christian West.

In the Arab World

The heartlands of Islam include cultures, for which, the issue of 'saving face' is critical. We find that Islam, like Judaism, emphasises outward performance to which status is attached. This is often referred to as the 'honour and shame' code. When I lived in the Middle East I remember an incident during Ramadan. The car I was being driven in scratched a car parked outside a house. At the time the owner was sitting on his veranda dressed in an immaculately starched white *gallabiyya* (Arab gown) and white skull-cap. His fingers were 'telling' his prayer beads and he looked the picture of devout spirituality during the holiest month of the Islamic calendar. When he heard the crunch his piety instantly evaporated.

He exploded into a fit of rage, grabbed an iron bar and hit our car then threatened to smash up us too.

Before you ask, I see this sort of incident, not as proof that Islam is 'demonic' but that this poor man had just had his car dented on a hot day when he was in his best clothes and didn't want to have to deal with it. If we must talk demons, how does this incident compare with 'road-rage' in the West? I recently heard a public confession to such behaviour by a well-known Christian speaker who was making the point 'we are all human'. Perhaps we need to keep an eye on any subtle attitude we may hold which says 'people like me are a little bit more human'.

The point is that because no two Muslim people are exactly alike we must accept the fact that their relationship with the 'religious' and 'social' aspects of their community are likely to be very different indeed. This means that part of the befriending process is to assess where your Muslim friend stands and the difference between what they say motivates them to practise Islam and what their behaviour might suggest is the reason. As with some Christians there can be a disparity between the two. So wherever the disparity is will likely be an area of felt need that only the gospel can address.

Sources:
1 www.africanecho.co.uk/africanechonews5-sept29.html https://en.wikipedia.org/wiki/History_of_slavery_in_the_Muslim_world

CHAPTER FIVE

Five Historical Barriers

We must talk to what the other means, not merely what they say. Refrain from being a mere debater and win the other to your meaning by accessing what lies behind their words.

When you hear strident things said, people can be in pain; so remember – they're hurting and be patient and reverent with what you do not understand.

Oswald Chambers, *The Shadow of an Agony*

It's inevitable that hurdles arise when we engage with someone from another culture. This is because their brain is wired differently to ours. But please note – these barriers reside in the mind-set of *both* us as Christians and our friend as a Muslim. They are often watching us watching them and this goes on through several invisible but sometimes tangible barriers which create an internal caution and even suspicion on both sides. These barriers hold us back from going out onto that 'bridge of friendship'.

The barriers are often rooted in the A-E-I-O-U we mentioned in chapter one; not least the *attitudinal* and *emotional* barriers. These tend to persist while we are starved of accurate *information* about Muslims and it is this that causes the lack of *understanding* we can suffer from.

The two-way barriers are a result of issues such as the...

1 negative interaction, which has happened between Christians and Muslims throughout history (i.e. the historical barrier)

2 difference in outlook, values and lifestyle (i.e. the cultural barrier)

3 sincerely held theological differences (i.e. the theological barrier)

4 terminology we prefer to use about spiritual and moral issues (i.e. the communicational barrier).

The barriers are not insurmountable and Muslims can be welcoming of the efforts of Christians to overcome them in the interests of gaining clarity between us. However, to cross the barriers does take a conscious effort on our part as we try to 'think into the shoes' of a Muslim.

St. Augustine of Hippo was one of the early Christians to define the Christian faith for the pagan mind, He ransacked secular thought for any points of communication so long as it didn't contradict the revealed truth of Scripture.

The ancient Hebrew Tabernacle in the Wilderness was furnished by melting down the pagan statuettes and pharaonic jewellery of Egypt. The gold of Egypt is still gold! Wherever truth is to be found it is the Lord's.

Augustine

Historical barrier

It's so easy to ignore history, but it's significant when engaging with someone from another cultural heritage. This became obvious one day on a university campus when an Iranian student was talking with an American Christian friend of mine. As the conversation got onto spiritual issues a barrier emerged in the mind of the Iranian. He became irate about the periods of history in which the West had bullied and damaged Muslim lands, leading (in his view) to the actions on 11 September 2001. My American friend was taken aback by the fact that this young Muslim was actually hurting as a result of world events, some of which happened centuries before he was even born. My friend sincerely apologised and asked forgiveness on behalf of the perpetrators of past atrocities against Muslims in the name of Christ.

The atmosphere became static with tension as tears appeared in the eyes of the Iranian Muslim who didn't know how to handle such a demonstration of the spirit of Jesus. It was a grace response. So what exactly is it that provokes Islamic anger? Here's a list of the sort of issues involved.

The Crusades (1095 - 1291AD)

This episode of history is remembered in the Muslim World as though it happened last year. The Crusades were a series of jihad-like military operations undertaken by armies sanctioned by the Church and representing 'Christendom'. These military campaigns occurred over a period of time in which European armies of 'Christian' mercenaries marched across Europe to re-take Jerusalem from the occupying Arab Muslims. As part of these operations, soldiers indulged in indiscriminate rape, murder and unwarranted brutality.

It's also true to say that Islamic history also features such episodes of brutality – including Muslim-on-Muslim. Nevertheless, the Crusades are an era in Christian history, which the modern church must somehow own as a carnal and therefore sinful part of our history. We need to adopt a more humble attitude and move out in the genuine spirit of Jesus Christ to Muslims.

A Muslim once remarked: "You (Christians) do not love the Muslims. But then you do not love one another either. Just look at the way you are divided in many denominations and you are fighting one another in Ireland". This remark shows how Muslims assume two things about the West.

I remind you that during the Crusades, Muslims were attacked by Christians who came from Europe. 70,000 were killed in one day. Yet no Muslim authority has ever written against Christianity. We have always made a distinction between the religion and those who sully its name. In the case of September 11 you in the West did not make that distinction.

Dr. Ahmad al-Tayyib (Grand Mufti of Al-Azhar University, Cairo)

Firstly that if someone is born in Algeria they are automatically 'Muslim'; likewise a non-Muslim born in Europe is automatically viewed as a 'Christian'.

Secondly many Muslim assumes that, if in Islam religion and state are the same thing, the same must be true in the West i.e. western politics is synonymous with Christianity.

The dismantling of the Ottoman Empire, 1924
The Ottoman Empire was the last vestige of Islamic greatness on the world stage. It went into decline as the widespread flowering of Islamic learning and culture began to disintegrate. This is a painful reality for many Muslims to accept. It was into this situation that the West intervened for a variety of reasons, triggering what appeared to be the carving up of the Ottoman Empire by western politicians, almost over a cup of coffee in European capitals. Hence Saddam Hussein's claim to Kuwait, which was based on borders known in the region, which the West had moved to suit the political agenda at that time.

The establishing of the State of Israel, 1948
Britain, France and America were key players in the formation of the 'political state' of Israel. Reformist Muslims are anti-Israel rather than anti-Semitic *per se*. We need to remember that Arabs themselves are Semites, which makes the tension in the Middle East more like a family squabble between first cousins over rights to a piece of 'holy' land.

It's also an open question as to why the other Arab States are conspicuous by their absence in terms of trying to bring resolution or receive Palestinian exiles and refugees. It seems the Palestinian people are left as pawns in a wider political game. Colin Chapman's book 'Whose Promised Land?' provides a helpful overview of the situation (see Appendix 5).

Evangelical Christians often confuse the political state of Israel with the Israel of biblical prophecy. This leads to problems, for example...

- How far is the behaviour of the Israeli government forces towards Palestinians worthy of the character of the God of Israel? How far can we call recent events, the 'fulfilment of biblical prophecy'? Take for instance John Pilger's documentary *'Palestine is still the Issue'*, which showed film footage of Israeli soldiers breaking the arms of Palestinian youths with boulders. In the same programme shown on 15th September 2002 there were scenes where Israeli soldiers had defecated and fouled furniture, walls and equipment in every room as they ransacked Palestinian buildings, which were used for children and young people's social activities.

  Or for example a male friend of mine who applied as a volunteer on a kibbutz was asked questioned before being assigned a kibbutz. He was told he would be posted according to his requirements i.e. did he want sex with girls, sex with men, drugs or alcohol. He would be assigned a placement accordingly.

- To what extent is the Old Testament injunction to care for the *'stranger in the midst'* (Lev.19:18,33) being carried out? We have to note the existence of significant human rights violations; racism; a hedonistic and atheistic society in which Christian medical workers report that one free abortion is available to all serving female Israeli soldiers during their military service.

- Clearly one of the biggest blockages to gaining the trust of Muslims is the fact that they perceive the West (i.e. including the Christian Church), to be endorsing and financially supporting the political State of Israel. The American government aid package to Israel runs at several million dollars a day. However, there is a way to embrace the significance of Bible prophecy about the spiritual reality of Israel and its people while standing up for biblical human rights and values with regard to the geographical reality of Israel/Palestine and its peoples today.

The Gulf Wars

In both Gulf Wars there was a victory against Muslims, by Muslims, with the help of non-Muslims. A unique combination that broke the understanding of Muslims that God will never allow non-Muslims to triumph over Muslims in battle; the fact that this happened centuries ago in Spain, and again in Kuwait, was a cause for understandable disquiet in the Muslim world.

Muslim world dependence on the West and East Asia

Muslim economies need foreign involvement and it's often the West and East Asia that are the providers of the expertise and technology Muslim countries need to function in the modern world. Yet most of them are critical of, what they see as, a morality of convenience, godless, greedy and materialistic. Assertive Muslims openly accuse the West of fostering a culture that is sex-crazed, pornographic, perverted and lust-intoxicated. While most Christians recognise what they are saying as having some validity particularly with the rise of online pornography, it must also be said that similar patterns exist but tend to be well hidden within Muslim societies.

Continued US presence in Saudi Arabia

Muslims are also critical of the continuing presence of American and allied military forces in Saudi, Turkey, Egypt and other key sites in the Middle East region. This is seen as a continuation of the Crusades, by people they refer to as *kufar* or infidels.

Islamic structures in the modern world

Although the Qur'an promises Muslims "the upper hand", their lands are often underdeveloped and disenfranchised, compared to the, so called, 'infidel' of the West and East Asia. While this causes anger amongst hard-line Islamic groups, it begs the question as to why this is the case. (see quote by Dr Zaki Badawi in Chapter 1).

This list of issues above leaves me with a profound sense of responsibility not to become 'salt in the wound' for a person from a Muslim family background who has grown up with certain urban myths about how the world works. I grew up in an African-Caribbean family which meant I absorbed many such myths about 'white people'. So whether a Muslim's views are rooted in things that are more imaginary than real, is beside the point. If the opinion is valid for them then to all intents and purposes it's 'real' for them. So to merely attack; ridicule; or trivialise will only help to dismantle the 'bridge of friendship' and undermine trust; which is the only place we can be more objective about our closely held values and assumptions about how the world works.

So a person's view of what has gone before in history affects the way they perceive the world. But this is only a segment of the wider influence on them that we call "culture". What is it and how does it affect us? This is where we turn next.

CHAPTER SIX

The Cultural Barrier

Muslim criticism of western civilization is not primarily a political confrontation. The real competition is that one is based on Islamic values and the other on materialism. Had western culture been based on Christianity, morality and faith, the modus operandi of the conflict would be different. But the only choice is between the divine principle of Islam and secular materialistic culture.

Khurshid Ahmad

In my early days of living in the Middle East the cheapest way to get from Egypt to Cyprus was by overnight ship. I was a post-graduate student in Cairo at the time and so saved enough money to travel. During the sailing I got talking to an Egyptian man and things were going well as we compared notes on all sorts of important issues. As time went on various people asked me for "ba'sheesh" (i.e. a tip for services rendered).

Problem was I hadn't budgeted for that so I couldn't give anything extra without running out of money myself. Eventually I became irritated with repeated requests so I said heatedly (in front of the man I was getting on so well with) "You're paid by the shipping company so why should I give you more?" My friend froze on the spot and would not continue the conversation but just walked away muttering under his breath.

The moral of the story is that two 'mind-maps' were clashing. Mine was a western one which said to me: "All tips are only optional upon excellent service beyond the call of duty", while the local 'mind-map' said to them: "Tips are obligatory regardless of how the service is performed because it's a way of trickling wealth down the pecking order and a way of looking after one another". This was an important lesson for me in the art of cross-cultural living.

"Culture" is an important barrier to be aware of when relating to people born into a Muslim family. The word "culture" is a complex one – easy to say but difficult to define. Most people tend to spot the influence of culture when they're on package holidays, when we spot things that are different or quaint or confusing, for example locals kissing on both

DEFINITIONS OF CULTURE

'Culture is an ordered way of life in which people do things together. It is any integrated system of learned behaviour patterns, characteristic of the members of a society, which are not the result of biological inheritance.' Malinowski

'Culture is an integrated system of beliefs (i.e. God, reality or ultimate meaning), of values (i.e. what is true, good, beautiful or normative), of customs (i.e. how to behave, relate to others, talk, pray, dress, work, play, trade, farm, eat, etc), and of institutions which express these beliefs, values and customs (i.e government, law courts, temples or churches, family, schools, hospitals, factories, shops, unions, clubs, etc) which binds society together and gives it a sense of identity, dignity, security and continuity.'

Source: Willowbank Report - Gospel & Culture, Lausanne Paper, No.2, Wheaton, 1978"

cheeks. However, we can fail to recognise the significance of culture, particularly when it comes to our own.

We will now look at what culture is and how it impacts the way we decide what is "normal". We will also say something about the pressing need to develop the skill of relating appropriately, to people from other cultures.

Respect for culture

Culture is a part of God's creative design for humankind and is an important biblical value. The variety of cultures is celebrated in the Bible where tribes, languages and peoples are listed (Rev.5:9). The apostle Paul, although often at odds with his own race over the issue of the gospel for the nations, was only too aware of his Jewish cultural roots. This affected him racially, educationally and spiritually (Phil.3:3-11). Culture also seems to be present in heaven as '*the kings of the earth bring their splendour into New Jerusalem*' (Rev.21:24). To relate to a Muslim with genuine respect for their culture will get us much further across the bridge of friendship, than merely being doctrinally correct. A Muslim is likely to notice what we are like, long before what we say. Our attitude will speak louder to Muslims than our words. To get this wrong can lead to serious problems.

A girl on a mission in the north of England accosted an elderly Muslim outside a public loo. It was summer time and she was wearing a skimpy tightly fitting vest and tight shorts. She shoved a tract at the Muslim and said "Jesus is the Son of God and died for your sins, if you repent and accept him into your life as your personal Saviour you can go to heaven".

The Muslim was furious. She was devastated and tearfully reported back to her group how hard Muslims are to evangelise. In reality she had broken every cultural rule in the book and had offended the Muslim and left him further away from the gospel than when she started.

Western cultures are no better or worse than Eastern cultures - just different. For example, it's interesting how British society which provides abortion on-demand reacts judgementally to issues such as female circumcision and arranged marriages.

An example of culture as the entry point for Christian witness is the fact that Islam can be seen, culturally and theologically as an 'Arabised reflection of Judaism'. This is due to its roots in Abraham and an Old

Testament Semitic mind-set. As such Islam affirms the Torah and has developed its own version of it – shari'a. It also venerates the Jewish prophets; its males are circumcised and it has a lunar calendar. The Five Pillars of Islam are rooted in Old Testament practice; and Muslim identity sees itself as being linked to the heritage of Abraham via the sons of Ishmael (i.e. the Arabs) who are a parallel to their ethnic and spiritual cousins the sons of Isaac (i.e. the Jews). So in several respects, as it is for the Jew, so it is for the Muslim.

> ...'even to this day whenever the old covenant is being read, the same veil covers their minds so they cannot understand the truth. And this veil can only be removed by believing in Christ...But whenever someone turns to the Lord, then the veil is taken away.' (2 Cor.3:14,16)

These similarities bring Muslims and Christians closer to one another than is comfortable for either. This is why Islam (albeit unwittingly) has the effect of preparing a Muslim to hear the good news by instilling into him or her, some of the basic building-blocks of the gospel. In this way, many Muslims live in a 'pre-evangelised' state. Just imagine if the Holy Spirit were to 'lift the floodgates' and move in power; we would see millions of Muslims swept into the Kingdom of God.

Should such an ingathering happen, Muslims could be the Gentiles who fulfil the Apostle Paul's predictions of a people who will *'provoke the Jews to jealousy'* (Rom.10:19; 11:11).

A Christian leader of a ministry among Jewish people told me how Jewish people – as sons of Isaac – have been coming to Christ worldwide in greater numbers than at any time in history and that these followers of Jesus are being approached by Muslims – particularly Arabs – (i.e. sons of Ishmael) and being asked to discuss the Bible and the claims of Christ. This is indeed a cultural access-point.

There are strengths and weaknesses, which normally come bundled up together. Thus people in the West tend to admire, rather guiltily, the concern (Muslims) show for the elderly, while being critical of the pressure on young people to conform to arranged marriages...both have a common root in respect for elders.

J & S Root

Because man is God's creation, some of his culture is rich in beauty and goodness. Because man is fallen, all of his culture is tainted with sin and some of it will be demonic.

The key issue is to look for the open doors for the gospel in other cultures. An excellent example of this is the apostle Paul in Athens (Acts 17) where he gave a superb cross-cultural open-air message, which maximised his access to the open door in their thinking, while minimising the possibility of the Greek hearers closing that door.

One way to understand the nebulous concept of "culture" is to ask what comes into your mind when you think of being French? Do you think of the Eiffel Tower, baguettes, kissing on both cheeks, fine cuisine, onions, good wine, the French language or the war time French Resistance. Of course these are only surface stereotypes, which are a caricature of real French culture, but it is a start.

EXAMPLE

Cement is made up of natural ingredients but its use is cultural e.g. a pavement or a minaret. Cotton is natural but its use is cultural e.g. pin-striped shirts or a sari.

What comes to your mind when you think of being whatever your nationality is? I'm British and I think of typical British things such as Welsh male voice choirs, Scottish Bag Pipes, English Morris dancing, Irish balads, monarchy, the last night of the Proms, candy floss, Pearly Queens, Fish & Chips and quaint country villages? The list is endless but they are still only surface observations. When we recognise how shallow these images are, and that culture is embedded in us like the layers of an onion, we can appreciate how we tend to caricature other cultures according to the observable behaviour rather than the deeper values, which are what really make them tick.

The inevitable contrast between cultures can become a clash if we are not careful. Here are some contrasts to look out for in Muslim cultures. Just ask yourself what are the implications of each of them and which are more biblical?

WESTERN CULTURE	EASTERN CULTURE
individualistic	corporate decision-making
efficiency-oriented	relationship-oriented
man-centred	God-centred in theory
equality of sexes	stricter segregation of roles
fragmented nuclear family	extended family
elderly institutionalised	elderly kept in family home
time-oriented	hospitality & relationship-oriented
relationships in leisure & work	relationships within the extended family
achievement focussed education	education by discipline & rote learning
personalised religion	communal religion
sacred/secular divide	God-aware worldview

How can I define my own culture?

It is always hardest to define our own culture. This is made harder because of the effect of 'globalisation', which is causing even traditional cultures to change rapidly and merge together with increasing inter-connectedness with other cultures. However, one way to identify your own culture at work is to ask questions such as…

- Is it 'the done thing' to talk to people on public transport? - if not why not? If it is, what topics are appropriate - why?

- As a teenager, what weight, were you expected to give to your parents' authority - why?

- What sort of relating is acceptable between unmarried people of the opposite gender - why?

- Australian people like to use nicknames instead of full names or titles – why?

- British people talk little about money but much about the weather – why?

- How would you describe British table manners? Where, with whom and how do you eat? Do you use utensils or your hands – why?

- New Zealand men traditionally like to be seen as macho - why?

- How do you spend your leisure time - why?

- Which relationships are most important to you - why?

- How do you prefer to communicate over distances - why?

- What is your feeling about punctuality?

- Is queuing important to you - If so why? If not, why not?

- Why do people tend to say "Fine!" when asked "How are you?"

How can I get a handle on Muslim cultures?

Muslim cultures are many and varied around the world, which means a Pakistani and an Arab Muslim can be as foreign to one another as a Briton and a German. Like Europeans, Muslims are divided by their different languages, traditional dress, food, history and general way of life.

Here are some aspects of Muslim culture, which are common to many parts of the Muslim world and are often found among the older generation of Muslims in the West as well as those who have arrived more recently and may be less culturally integrated.

- Indirect negotiation i.e. talking round the houses before coming to the point (see Gen.23)

- Respect for elders and old age (see Lev.19:32)

- Segregation of genders

- Extended family with male priority - grandfather, father, oldest son, then mother

- A high concept of God (see Ex.34:1-8)

- Modesty of dress - males cover their belly-button to knee, females from neck to wrists and ankles.

- Modesty of behaviour

- Official abstinence from alcohol and pork

- God-centred mind-set

- Respect for religious observance (see Mt.5:17-20; 6:1-6)

- Religion as a topic of conversation

- Religious phraseology - see Jn.20:26

- Corporate consciousness - little privacy or individual decision-making

- Family & relationship-oriented networks

- Prescriptive rather than analytical learning - (n.b. "Why?" is an un-Islamic question, which may explain the struggle for Muslim economies to develop technologically.)

- Saving of 'face' or dignity - not to be belittled in front of others

- Supernatural and magical awareness with natural/spiritual continuum

- Leisure time is family oriented

- Accepting of 'fate' as God's will - greater resignation to circumstances

- The traditional payment of dowry usually paid in jewellery, money or property is still practiced

Islam is both religion and lifestyle

Muslim proverb

Cross-cultural do's & don'ts

The following points are aimed at relating to more conservative and therefore devout Muslims. As culture is such a difficult issue to pin-down, many of the points may not apply even to some practicing Muslims, so rather than assuming that these are hard and fast rules, it's best to be sensitive and, when in doubt, just ask them. Most of the points are totally irrelevant for younger, more westernised Muslims, whose values will be a mixture of Muslim and British cultures.

Don'ts

1   Don't try to compliment or criticise Muhammad or Islam - be tactful but honest.

2   Don't refer to the Qur'an as poetry. In Islam poets are generally thought to be demon-inspired.

3   If your Muslim friend is devout, don't play music (especially modern gospel) because music is seen in Islam, as associated with immorality. Remember that neither music nor singing is part of Muslim worship, although chanting is not seen as singing.

4   Don't use your left hand to eat with or pass food to a devout Muslim. The left hand is taboo as it is the 'toilet' hand in many Muslim cultures.

5   Don't offer alcohol, pork, pork products or anything made from animal oils. All these break the halal law of Islam.

6   Don't point the sole of your foot at a Muslim. This is insulting.

7   Don't tell jokes unless you know your Muslim friend really well. Jokes often backfire cross-culturally and can lead to misunderstanding.

8   Don't ask about the spouse of your Muslim friend as this can be taken to be odd and intrusive. It is better to ask generally "How is the family?"

9   Don't try to talk to a Muslim while they are eating unless they initiate it. Muslims tend to eat first and talk later.

10 Don't ask to use the toilet in a Muslim's home if at all possible. As with Gentiles to Jews, non-Muslims present an uncertainty in the area of ritual hygiene.

11 Don't mishandle the Bible or Qur'an by putting either of them on the floor if at all possible. Muslims normally keep them wrapped up and in a high place.

12 Don't write or underline the Bible or Qur'an you use to discuss with your friend.

13 Don't compliment a devout Muslim parent on the looks or abilities of their child. They may believe that this will attract the attention of the 'evil eye' through envy.

14 Don't discuss religion near an unclean place e.g. rubbish or toilet.

15 Don't say anything, which is openly supportive of the political state of Israel. It is better to refer to it as Palestine.

16 Don't smile and laugh with people of the opposite gender.

17 Don't point directly at someone if you can help it.

18 Don't assume you know what a Muslim believes - always ask.

Do's

1 Do enter a room and greet people of lower status first, then work your way up to the most senior in age or prestige.

2 Do shake hands with people but don't linger with people of the opposite gender.

3 Do greet everyone. A Muslim proverb says 'Guilt slips away through the hands' which refers to the social importance of establishing peace in relationships when there has been misunderstanding.

4 Do take time to ask after "the family" in detail.

5 Do be ready to be embraced by an Asian or kissed on both cheeks by an Arab. Arabs also may linger holding your hand long after shaking it.

6 Do remove your shoes in the home of a devout Muslim. Wear clean socks.

7 Do sit with people of your own gender. The seat nearest the door is the humblest place. You may be invited to a more prominent chair (Lk.14:10).

8 Do sit with good, if slightly formal, posture and keep your feet on the floor as opposed to slouching.

9 Do use both hands to offer anything. To use one hand communicates half-heartedness and lack of respect for the person.

10 Do be objective about the moral failings of your own nation and express interest in their perceptions of it.

11 Do avert your eyes from staring into the eyes of a Muslim of the opposite gender. Too much eye contact is seen as forward and flirtatious.

12 Do try to remember to enter a room right foot first as this may be the custom of your friend.

13 Do excuse yourself to go and wash your hands before handling a Bible or Qur'an. Always hold either book in the right hand to show respect for it and carry it in a covering.

14 Do remove any statues, crosses or Jewish six-pointed stars from your home or jewellery in the presence of a devout Muslim.

15 If you have a dog, do lock it away and remove their food bowls because dogs are seen by devout Muslims as unclean.

We have seen that – unlike the sacred/secular divide in western societies – Islam is woven into the way a Muslim thinks and lives, whether she is a practising in the strict sense of the word. It's similar to the way British people have traditionally valued having a 'stiff upper lip' which helps them to 'keep calm and carry on' in difficult circumstances.

Our behaviour is an outworking of our 'worldview' of life; our 'belief' about life; and what we most 'value' in life. So like the Judeo-Christian heritage affecting the values in western societies, so Islam has become an overlay of localised Muslim cultures. Like Judaism, it's helpful to think of Islam as more than a religion because it has become a way of life.

Yes Islam is a religion and we need to be aware of what the core teaching is; what Muslims make of it; and how to relate the gospel to people who are starting with those beliefs and assumptions. This is where we turn in the next chapter.

CHAPTER SEVEN

The Theological Barrier

All fundamental differences between Islam and Christianity are rooted in the perception of God. Islam perceives God to be a being who does not seek relationship and is unknowable while Christianity perceives God to be a person who came into Eden calling for man. He has been actively seeking relationship with people ever since.

Jay Smith (adapted)

Although Islam is a 'religion' doctrine is not the primary issue when it comes to forming a 'spiritual friendship' with someone from a Muslim family. The aim is not to have fights in an atmosphere of combat and conflict about what Muslims are supposed to believe, so much as to compare notes with them about how their beliefs affect their lives. The point is that the 'worldview' created by Islamic doctrine shapes a Muslim's values and behaviour to differing degrees.

The Muslim worldview is based on a prescriptive set of required beliefs. The western worldview has increasingly moved away from the moral and spiritual foundations derived from the Judeo-Christian Bible heritage. I still find it ironic how many people in western societies can be intolerant of the very heritage which gave it the value of tolerance in the first place.

The different perspectives on life held by Christians and Muslims gives rise to huge misunderstandings; the problem is made worse when we don't even realise this difference is there. Someone once said: 'Muslims and Christians are playing on the same games board. The problem is Christians are playing chess while Muslims are playing draughts'.

Like many Westerners who have never held a Qur'an but still have definite views about it, your Muslim friend may have never seen the Bible in their own language but will likely have all sorts of opinions about it.

We eventually have to face these doctrinal contrasts which are significant. It's just that they are not necessarily the first thing we need to focus on. This is why I have left the theological barrier till now. If we can't overcome the first three barriers we will probably never earn the right, in a Muslim's eyes, to address these issues with them in a helpful way. Those who dive straight into the doctrinal issues – which will be very close to a devout Muslim's heart – are inviting a defensive reaction.

So what follows is a comparison of Islam and Christian teaching on a variety of issues.

MUSLIM BELIEFS	CHRISTIAN BELIEFS

Religion for God

'If anyone desires a religion other than Islam, it shall not be accepted from him and in the world to come he shall surely be among the losers' (S3.85) n.b. Muhammad is a bringer of religion.

Relationship with God

'*Neither is there salvation in any other: for there is none other name under heaven given among men, whereby we must be saved.*' (Acts 4:12) n.b. Jesus came to bring, not religion but salvation.

Identity of Allah

There is only one High God of the universe who is worshipped inadequately by Jews and Christians alike. '*Our God and your God is One*'. (S29.46; 3.64)

The Qur'an's understanding of God is not the same as the Bible's, but Muslims are still open to general revelation.

See 'Allah' in the 'Useful Explanations'.

Identity of Allah

Although controversial among Christians, the name *Allah* comes from *El-illah*. This means *High God* and was known in the Middle East long before Islam. Linguistically Allah is related to the Hebrew version El of the Old Testament (e.g. El-ohim, El-Shaddai).

Allah is the only word available to millions of Arabic speaking Christians. Allah is the God of the Bible with the proviso that Muslims' understanding of Him is faulty.

Inspiration of Scripture

The very words of the Qur'an were revealed to Muhammad. He became like a typewriter and recited them to scribes. His thought and ideas were not involved (S29.48).

It is unnecessary and wrong to examine the "sources" of the Qur'an. Because the Qur'an was received in Arabic it must be recited and read in Arabic.

Translations are not valued and only regarded as giving the general meaning.

Inspiration of Scripture

The writers of the Bible were inspired by the Holy Spirit (1 Pt.1:21). It shows the individual personality of the writers. In this sense the Bible is the Word of God and entrusted through men.

Although the Bible writers were inspired, we are encouraged to compare and search the Scriptures.

The Old Testament was written in Hebrew and Aramaic, the NT in Greek. A translation of the Bible is just as much the Bible as the Hebrew original. The point is intelligibility of the truth not veneration of the text.

MUSLIM BELIEFS	CHRISTIAN BELIEFS
The Eternal Tablet The verbal revelations of Torah, Psalms, Gospel and Qur'an come from a template in heaven (S85.22). This is also called 'The Mother of the Book' (S13.39; 43.4).	**The Eternal Tablet** Jesus is the dynamic equivalent of the 'Eternal Tablet'. He is the Word of God who was with God from eternity (Jn.1:1-2; Heb.1:1). Islam teaches that nothing dwells with God, but the Eternal Tablet contradicts that.
Transcendence & Sovereignty of God God is greater than all our ideas about Him. He is Lord of the Worlds (S.1), the Creator and Sustainer of the universe (S3.189). At the same time he is nearer to man than his jugular vein (S50.16). God is almighty and predestines everything in the universe, including both good and evil.	**Transcendence & Sovereignty of God** Christians have a similar belief in God's sovereignty but stress God's nearness ('The Kingdom of God is at hand'). God is available to all of us in Christ. Christians try to keep the balance between God's sovereignty and man's free will and responsibility. However less stress is put on the idea of God's determining of everything and almost none on God decreeing evil.
Man as a creature The relationship of man to God is as a servant to his Master.	**Man as a creature** Man was created in the *image and likeness of God* (Gen.1:27). This image is spoiled but not destroyed. God reached out to make us his children in Christ. We believe that man was created to *tend the earth and subdue it* (Gen.1:28).

MUSLIM BELIEFS

CHRISTIAN BELIEFS

Man as a sinner

When Adam sinned, it was personal to him. It did not amount to a "Fall" for the whole human race.

Everyone is born sinless with a clean sheet before God. Sin is a fault (S4.111; 6.120; 24.11). We must try harder if we sin.

The Law of God

God's requirements are contained in the law (shari'a) and the most important are the Five Pillars of Islam.

Creation of the world

Mankind was created in Paradise (janna). He was banished to earth (S2.36).

Various numbers of days are given for the creation. A cluster of days is also mentioned. This allows for a 'day' being millions of years and therefore it is sufficiently vague as to be compatible with evolution theory.

Man was created carnivorous and cattle were created for man to eat (S6.142; 16.5).

Adam & Eve became aware that they were naked after they sinned (S20.121). The Qur'an also suggests they were clothed before the fall (S7.27).

Man as a sinner

Adam's sin affected the whole human race (Ps.51:5; Rom.3:23; 5:12; 1 Cor.15:22).

Original sin means we inherit a fallen human nature from our parents. We sin because we are sinners. We are born in alienation from God and need reconciling back into relationship with him.

The Law of God

God's basic requirements are revealed in the 10 Commandments, which cover our relationship to God and our neighbour.

Creation of the world

Mankind was created on earth in the Garden of Eden. (Gen.2:8) and later banished from it. However we understand the "days" of Genesis, the earth came before the Sun, which may rule out a 'big bang'.

Man and animals were created vegetarian (Gen.1:29-30). Originally there was no death and suffering.

Mankind was created naked and not ashamed (Gen.2:25). Shame is a human response to sin.

MUSLIM BELIEFS	CHRISTIAN BELIEFS
Salvation Only by submission to God and Qur'an can we escape the 'blazing fire' (S3.85). Salvation is by falah (self-effort or positive achievement) (S23.102-103).	**Salvation** This is only possible through Jesus Christ (Jn.14:6; Acts 4:12). It is by grace through faith (Eph.2:8-9.
Mission Spreading Islam is called dahwa (invitation). This may be by many methods i.e. educational, cultural, community development or by force where necessary.	**Mission** Spreading of the gospel is with gentleness (Lk.10:3,36-37) and respect (1 Pt.3:15). No earthly weaponry is used (2 Cor.10:3-5) and the response is voluntary.
The Fall of Man Satan enticed Adam and Eve (S7.20-21; 20:120). The 'mistake' of disobeying God only affected Adam. Man is not a sinner, just weak (S4.28) and rebellious (S96.6). The couple were given 'raiment' but no mention of this being skins (S7.26). Work, sweat and struggle were part of the original creation order (S90.4). Death is not an enemy it is part of the original created order.	**The Fall of Man** The serpent enticed Eve, denying she would die (Gen.3:1-5). Adam's sin somehow entered the bloodline and gene pool. All are now born with the sin principle in them. God provided garments of skins (Gen.3:21). 'Painful toil' and sweat are a product of the curse (Gen.3:17,19). Death is an enemy resulting from the fall of man (Gen.2:17; 3:19; Rom.5:12; 17:1; 1 Cor.15:21-22,26).
Flesh/spirit struggle Compromise is allowed for with sensual and physical aspects of life	**Flesh/spirit struggle** Struggle against the flesh is expected (Rom.5-8; Gals.5:16). This is only possible through Jesus Christ (Jn.14:6; Acts 4:12). It is by grace through faith (Eph.2:8-9)

MUSLIM OBJECTIONS
TO THE GOSPEL

CHRISTIAN RESPONSES
TO MUSLIM OBJECTIONS

Supremacy of Muhammad over Christ

Muhammad is seen as the final and universal prophet, superior to all others, including Jesus, who Muslims respect but think of only as a prophet sent to the Jews (S3.49; Is.49:6).

Muhammad is called the 'unlettered one' and is seen as the fulfilment of Messianic prophecies.

Bible texts used by some Muslims to refer to Muhammad include …

- Gen.17:20 - one from Ishmael's house taken to be a reference to Muhammad

- Deut.33:2 - seen as reference to Arabs

- Ps.45 - is seen as ode to Muhammad

- Ps.149:6-9 - is seen as Islamic conquest

- Is.42:1-4; 53; 63:1-6; Hag.2:7; Mat.3:3; 21:43-44; Mk.1:7 are seen as references to Muhammad.

- Jn.4:21; Jude 14:15 - are seen as referring to Islam

Supremacy of Muhammad over Christ

Biblical prophecy consistently points to a Jew as Messiah who was to come. For example Gen.49:10 shows that the obedience of the nations was to be to one from the house of Judah. Christians believe that the references opposite have been lifted and reapplied to Muhammad, who came after Jesus, the one they really refer to.

Everything was created through Christ, who was pre-existent before creation (Gen.1:26; 3:22; 11:7; Mic.5:2; Jn.1:1-3, 10; 3:13; 6:62; 8:35,58; 17:5, 24; Rom.11:36; 1 Cor.8:6; Cols.1:16-17; Heb.1:2)

Jesus is the Messiah of the OT (Is.7:14 & Mat.1:22-23; Mic.5:2 & Mat.2:1-6; Is.61:1-2 & Lk.4:16-21; Is.52:13 & Ac.8:29-35; Ps. 16:8-11 & Ac.2:22-36). There is no biblical support for Muhammad.

MUSLIM OBJECTIONS
TO THE GOSPEL

The Holy Spirit
The Qur'an mentions the Holy Spirit (S2.87; 17.85; 70.4; 78.38; 97.4). However Muslims see an impersonal revealer (S16.102; 42.52). A common text used is Jn.14:16,17,26 where the word *Parakletos* (comforter) is claimed to be a reference to Muhammad. Muslim tradition teaches that Christians changed the text from *Parakultos*, which is the equivalent of *ahmad* (the praised one), which is the Arabic root of the name *Muhammad* (S61.6).

Supremacy of the Qur'an over the Bible
The Qur'an teaches respect for the Bible (S3.84; 4.136). Muslims have only a polite respect for Torah and Injil as they believe the Qur'an contains the truth more perfectly. Yet the Qur'an persistently misquotes the Bible. For example...

- Abraham's father was not Azar as in S6.74, but Terah (Gen.11:26).
- Pharaoh's daughter adopted Moses, not his wife as in S28.7-9 (see Ex.2:5-20).
- Aaron's sister Miriam was not Mary the mother of Jesus as in S19.27-28 (see Ex.15:20 & Num.26-59).
- Pharaoh did not instruct Haman to build the Tower of Babel, as in Sura 28.38. It happened in Babylon generations earlier (Gen.11:1-9).
- Joseph didn't have his shirt torn by Potiphar's wife, he fled the temptation

CHRISTIAN RESPONSES
TO MUSLIM OBJECTIONS

The Holy Spirit
From earliest church history has come the definitive statement 'I believe in the Holy Spirit, the Lord and giver of life, who proceeds from the Father and the Son; who together with them is worshipped and glorified' (Nicene Creed). See Gen.1:2; Rom.8; Eph.4:30; 1 Cor.6:19. The Holy Spirit is personal, active and involved in God's world.

Supremacy of the Bible over the Qur'an
While some Muslims see the Old and New Covenants as contradictory e.g. *'An eye for an eye and a tooth for a tooth'* in contrast to *'Love your enemies'*, the Bible is a 'developmental' revelation through history. However, the Qur'an actually does contradict itself. For example...

- God will never forgive associating a partner with Him (S4.116), yet Abraham did this very thing (S6.76-78).
- The Qur'an claims to confirm both Tawrat & Injil (S3.3) yet It contradicts the central doctrines of Jesus' being divine, the death of Christ, his atonement for sin, and the resurrection.
- The Qur'an denies the crucifixion in S4.157-158, then affirms it (S3.55).
- The Qur'an is positive about Christians (S29.46) as well as negative (S5.54)
- The Qur'an says creation took 6 days (S25.59) then 8 days (S41.9-12).

MUSLIM OBJECTIONS
TO THE GOSPEL

CHRISTIAN RESPONSES
TO MUSLIM OBJECTIONS

The Person of Christ

Jesus is a respected prophet of Islam. He is seen as a created being (S3.59) and a prophet to the Jews. He was born of a virgin (S19.19-21). He was superior to all other men (S66.12). He is *Kalimat Allah* (Word of God) and *Ruhallah* (Spirit of God) (S4.171) *Word of Truth* (S19.34) and *Holy* (S19.19). He is known by Muslims as *The miracle working prophet* (S3.49).

Muhammad's role was to correct the distorted Jewish and early Christian error about Jesus. *'If the All-merciful has a son, then I am the first to serve him'* (S43.81). (See Appendix 1)

The Person of Christ

Jesus himself claimed the title 'Son of God' (Mt.2:11; 16:13-17; Mk.5:6-7 Jn.1:1; 9:35-38;11:4; 20:28). "Son of God" is a spiritual-title – not a physical description.

'Son of' is a Middle Eastern phrase showing an inseparable connection e.g. the expression "son of the streets" in Arabic. See Psalm 2; 22 & 24.
The tradition that Jesus is "only" a prophet is based on the Qur'an's Arabic expression *'inna maa'*. This can be translated either "only" or "certainly", so Muhammad would be insisting that Jesus was "clearly" a prophet of God, aiming to convince Jews who were rejecting Jesus altogether. It makes little sense for him to say that Jesus is "only" a prophet as some Muslims claim.

The Corruption of the Bible

The Qur'an is the revelation of God's will. It is the final pure and verbatim revelation from God. The Bible allows for human personality and therefore error. An Islamic tradition says that it has also been tampered with and changed (S2.59; 7.162). This concept of "corruption" is called *tahrif*, which comes from *harrafa* in Arabic.

Yet nowhere does the Qur'an actually say that *tahrif* applies to the Bible (S4.46). Rather than stating that the Bible has been changed, the accusation in the verse was that certain Jews misrepresented their own Scripture and also Muhammad's words (S2.75).

The Integrity of the Bible

The Bible is the revelation of God Himself. Its inspiration is not verbatim but truth poured through human personalities.

Muslims are required to believe the previous holy books (S2.136; 4.136), which the Qur'an affirms (S10.37; 35.31). Humans cannot change God's words according to the Qur'an (S6.34; 10.64).

- When was the Bible changed? It could not have been before 622 AD as the Qur'an affirms the Bible was the accurate Word of God at that date (S2.136; 4.136). The earliest biblical manuscripts in the British Museum date from before

MUSLIM OBJECTIONS
TO THE GOSPEL

(The Corruption of the Bible continued)
The 'Gospel of Barnabas' was written in the 17th Century by an Italian convert to Islam. It was discovered in Amsterdam in 1709 and this is hailed by some Muslims as the true *Injil* (Gospel). It is a major source of the Muslim objection to Jesus' deity; his death and the Trinity. However, it has serious inaccuracies about history, geography and even contradicts the Qur'an; a point that gets overlooked.

Muslims believe the Bible is now *mansukh* (redundant or superseded) by Qur'an.

CHRISTIAN RESPONSES
TO MUSLIM OBJECTIONS

(The Integrity of the Bible continued)
Muhammad and there is no change. If God preserved the Qur'an from corruption, for 1,400 years, why would he not also preserve the Bible, which the Qur'an affirms as being protected by God?

- Where was the Bible changed? Hundreds of manuscripts in a dozen ancient languages have existed since before 622 AD. All agree with current manuscripts. No one could have altered all the originals in the world and then made our modern translation the same corrupted version.

- Who changed it? Why would Jews or Christians want to change the Bible?

- Why did God not permit Muslim scholars to save the original? Nowhere does the Qur'an state this; in fact it states the opposite (S10.64).

Four Gospels
Why do Christians have four Gospels today when there was only one true Gospel?

Four Gospels
God used individual personalities, which gives the four Gospels different perspectives on Jesus – who is 'the gospel'. This is integral to the truth expressed through them.

MUSLIM OBJECTIONS
TO THE GOSPEL

CHRISTIAN RESPONSES
TO MUSLIM OBJECTIONS

The Trinity

The Islamic view of God is governed by the concept of *tawhid* (the unity of God i.e. *"Allah il-waheed"* - God is one).

Some Muslims even think that Christians believe in three gods (i.e. God the Father, Mary the Mother & Jesus their offspring by a physical relationship) (S9:30-31).

The Angel Gabriel's announcement to Mary is taken by some Muslims to be a sexual reference i.e. '*The Holy Spirit will come upon you and the power of the Highest shall overshadow you and the thing to be born of you shall be called the Son of God*' (Lk.1:31).

This impression is understandable when we think of the traditional Roman Catholic image of the Madonna & Child. This is shirk (idolatry by equating something with God).

The three speakers in the Qur'an are God, the angel and Muhammad. Where God is speaking, he mostly uses the first person plural expression "We". Some scholars believe this is not the 'royal we' but came from the OT Scriptures which Muhammad may have been drawing on. A fact that helped prepare Arabs for the idea of Trinity.

The Trinity

Christians agree with Muslims that it is blasphemous to suggest that God physically sired Jesus. The Trinity is not three gods but one God revealed in three persons. The monotheistic root of Islam is rooted in the Arabic for 'one' (ahad) – solitary unity. This contrasts with the Hebrew for 'one' (echad) – corporate unity. If Jews (who were 'mono-theistic') recognised Jesus as a member of the divine community, so can Muslims. (See 'Gospel for Muslims', by Steve Bell, chapter 6, pg114-115)

The Trinity is revealed throughout the Bible. It is not the later invention of Christians. The 'oneness' of God is seen in Deuteronomy 6:4 biblical. 'Hear O Israel, the Lord our Lord is one Lord'. (see also Gen.1:25, Deut.4:32).

The concept is grasped by revelation not intellect but the following might help you:

- To be 'living' God needs to be able to speak (Jesus the Word) and have a spirit (Holy Spirit). This describes God's triune nature.

- The godhead is more like a family firm of three directors

- Humans are a trinity: spirit, mind & body

- Water comes in three forms - liquid, solid (ice) or gas (steam)

- An egg is a trinity of yoke, white & shell

MUSLIM OBJECTIONS
TO THE GOSPEL

CHRISTIAN RESPONSES
TO MUSLIM OBJECTIONS

The Crucifixion

The instinct of Muslims is to protect Jesus from the social 'shame' of a death by crucifixion. He is seen as a prophet of Islam and so must be esteemed. The Cross is therefore an insult to the Islamic aspiration of honour, power and prestige.

Hence why a Muslim tradition says Judas died in Jesus' place and God made him look like Jesus. *'They killed him not nor crucified him, but so it was made to appear...Allah raised him to himself'*. (S4.157-158).

The Qur'an does however refer to Jesus as the 'Lamb of God' (S3.39) in agreement with John 1:29. It also agrees with the sacrifice of Abraham's son (S37.107), though tradition says it was Ishmael not Isaac. This is celebrated as Eid Al-Adha (Sheep Feast), also called Eid Al-Kibir. This is atonement by blood as found in Numbers 19:1-10.

The Crucifixion

Muhammad also suffered (though not as severely as Jesus) so a prophet of Islam can suffer. (see Bill Musk's quote, page 62)

If God put someone else on the Cross instead of Jesus it would be deception and so a violation of his character.

Muslims understand S19.32-34 as saying God took Jesus directly to heaven but he will return to die and be raised to life – why then and not now? The Qur'an contradicts this in S4.157-158 by saying God 'caused Jesus to die' and raised him.

Biblical prophecies and Jesus' own predictions specify that it would be him who would die on the Cross (see Is.52:13-53:12; Ps.22; Mat.20:17-19; 26:2,28,31-32,56; Lk. 23:33; Jn.20:27; Cols.1:22; 1 Pt.1:18-19; Heb.9:13- 14).

THINK OF IT LIKE THIS...

The parallel of Jesus in Islam is not Muhammed but the Qur'an (i.e. the Qur'an is the 'word' made book while Jesus is the Word made flesh).

The parallel of Muhammed in Christianity is not Jesus but Mary (i.e. both Muslims and Christians see these two as carrying the 'word of God' into the world).

What Islam denies Muslims

1 *The truth of original sin*   This becomes "human weakness" or "mistakes" to be corrected.

2 *The availability of grace*   God has no desire for relationship. There is only taqdir (predetermination). A Muslim lives negotiating with God in the hope of doing better in future.

3 *Repentance*   A Muslim prays and hopes for self-improvement (i.e. spiritual DIY).

4 *Personal forgiveness*   There is no heart cleansing, only ritual purity. God may act with mercy on Judgement Day but He may not.

5 *Salvation*   This is seen as when God comes to our aid in the pressures of life like the deliverances sung about by the Psalmist David.

6 *Relationship with God*   This is fear and awe towards a distant God.

7 *The New Birth*   Muslims see no need of this, so it remains a redundant concept.

8 *Assurance of heaven*   Only fearful awaiting of Judgement Day hoping all will be well. Heaven is a sensuous male abode where women are free to all. n.b. How comfortable is your Muslim friend with the idea that their spouse could be ravished by others in paradise?

9 *Covenant-keeping God*   God is arbitrary and unpredictable.

THINK OF IT LIKE THIS...

'The Black Stone'

The Ka'aba is built on a rock formation, which has a black chunk of meteorite stone built into one corner. This is worn smooth, which has given rise to the tradition that this is the result of centuries of kissing and touching by Muslim pilgrims. Jesus is the cornerstone of the church (Eph 2:20). He is therefore the equivalent 'Black Stone' of the Christian faith. The Bible encourages worshippers of God to venerate Him when it says *'Kiss the Son so He will not be angry with you...'*. (Psalm 2)

Christ in the Qur'an

Acknowledgement to *Carey College* booklet series

When enquiring Muslims read the Qur'an, it can act as a stepping-stone to the truth of Christ. This is possible because there are significant details about Jesus in the Qur'an. He is repeatedly referred to as *"Isa ibn Miryam"* (Jesus son of Mary). Muhammad seemed to defend Jesus against the claim that he was illegitimate.

> *As a prophet rejected by his own people, the Qur'anic Jesus (Isa) looks a lot like Muhammad, who was at first rejected by the people of Mecca.*
>
> Kenneth L. Woodward

Jesus is given an eminent position in the Qur'an, where he is even superior to Muhammad himself. Jesus' supernatural character and holiness are made clear. Anyone insulting Jesus or Mary is warned (S4.155-156). One example of the high honour given to Jesus in the Qur'an is as follows…

That is our argument which we bestowed
upon Abraham as against his people.
We raise up in degrees whom We will;
Surely your Lord is All-wise, All-knowing.
And We gave to him Isaac & Jacob
And Noah We guided before and his seed
David & Solomon, Job & Joseph
Moses & Aaron -
Even so we recompense the good-doers -
Zachariah & Yehya, JESUS & Elijah;
Each was of the righteous;
Ishmael & Elisha, Jonah & Lot
Each one We preferred before all beings'.
(S6.83-86)

Kenneth Cragg refers to Jesus as a diadem set in a tiara of prophetic jewels. Old Testament characters such as Abraham, are listed as 'types' of the Messiah; for example Isaac and Jacob, David and Solomon are types of the "kingly" aspect of Christ. Job and Joseph are types of the suffering Christ, while Moses and Aaron are types of the law-giving and high-priestly aspect of Christ. Elijah (1 Kgs.17:17-24), Ishmael (Gen.21:14-19), and Elisha (2 Kgs.4:32-37) are all types of the resurrected aspect of Christ.

All this can help the stepping-stone effect for enquiring Muslims, by helping them to press on from Qur'an to Bible, in order to find the answers to the questions the Qur'an poses about Jesus.

There is enough material about Jesus in the Qur'an to lead a Muslim enquirer well on the way to faith in Jesus. When you are comparing the Bible and Qur'an with a Muslim friend, it's helpful to find the references to Jesus, where possible. Here are some examples:

1 **Jesus' Birth:** S3.35-51; 19.22-34; 21.91 – Mat.1:18-25, 2:1-23; Lk.1:26-80

2 **Jesus' Miracles:** S3.49, 5.113-118 – Mat.14:13-21,15;32-38, 26:17-29

3 **Jesus' Teaching:** S3.50-53, 5.119-121, 19:30-33 – Mat.5:1- 7:28

4 **Jesus' Death & Ascension:** S2.87;3.55; 4.157-159; 5.19,120; 19.33 – Mat.26-27; Jn.12:31-34; Ac.2:22-24; 1 Cors.15:20-28

5 **Jesus' Titles & Descriptions:** Why not work through this list with a Muslim friend and discuss the implications of the superlative titles and the references given to Jesus in the Qur'an.

- He is Creator of Life (S3.49: 5.113) n.b. he was existing before life began – Jn.1:4

- He is the Messiah, i.e. promised by all the prophets and a prophet promised from among the Jews (S3.45; 4.171; 5.19; 9.30) – Deut.18:18

- He is a sign from God (S3.50; 19.21; 23.50; 46:61) – Mat.24:30-31; 25:31-46

- He came for Israel (S3.49) and all nations (S21.91) – Jn.1:9,10,29; 3:16-17; 4:42

- His coming is significant now and in eternity (S3.45; 43.61)

- He is blessed (S19:31) – Mat.21:9; Lk.13:35

- He is a mercy from God (S19:21) – Lk.1:76-78

- The Spirit of God was on him (S2.253) - Mat 3:16-17

- He is the Word of Truth (S19.34) – Jn.1:17, 14:6

- He is an example (S43.57-59) – Jn.13:15

- He is illustrious and held in honour (S3.45) – Mat.25:31,32; Jn.17:5,24

- He is the Word of God (S3.39, 45; 4.171)…n.b. a 'word' is equal to a 'thought' or the 'mind' and soul itself; it is the closest thing to the speaker – Gen.1; Is.43:12

- He is one of the *'nearest to God'* (S3.45) – Jn.14:6; 20:17; Acts 7:55, 56

- He is the Spirit of God (S2.87, 253; 4:171; 5.113; 15.29; 21.91) – Mat.12:15-28; Acts 10:38

- He was an apostle or messenger of God (S2.253; 10.47) – Jn.6:29, 9:4, 12:44-50

The meaning of 'Son of God'

- Jesus was born of a virgin (S19.16-35). God did this by the Holy Spirit (S21.91).

- The father 'role' is taken by God who initiated the conception (S19.21-22).

- The biblical term "begotten" (Jn.3:16) is not helpful to a Muslim as it can give the impression that God physically fathered Jesus like a human being. The Greek says "mono-genesis", which means God's 'only born'. God sent Christ 'The Word of God' via the natural birth process of conception, gestation and delivery in order that *'The Word'* should *'become flesh and live for a while among us'* (Jn.1:14). See also Mat.1:18-23; Lk.1:26-35

- Jesus came out from the corporate unity of the godhead. He came from God who is the 'source' or origin (*assnad* in Arabic).

- Jesus existed as the 'Word of God' before he came to earth (S3.49, 5.113) – Jn.1:1-14; Heb.1:1-13

The Crucifixion of Jesus

Although the Qur'an appears to deny the crucifixion (S4.157-158) it also affirms Jesus' death and raising up to God (S3.55; 19.33-34). Many Muslims say this will happen at the end of the world – but there is no justification for this. Historic evidence for the crucifixion is found in the secular writings of Pliny, Tacitus and Josephus who were alive at the time.

'Now there was.... A man Jesus, a wise man if it be lawful to call him a man for he was a doer of wonderful works and a teacher of all who receive the truth with pleasure. He drew over to himself Jews and Gentiles. He was the Christ. Then Pilate at the suggestion of the principal one amongst us, had him condemned to the cross. Those that loved him did not forsake him and he appeared to them alive again the third day as the divine prophets had foretold (see Isaiah 53: Psalm 16:8-11) *these and ten thousand other wonderful things concerning him. The tribe of Christians, so named from him, are not extinct to this day.'*
Josephus (Antiquities of the Jews Vol.18 3:3)

This chapter has at least given you an outline and overview of the core of Islamic teaching and how it compares with the Bible's teaching. Rather than seeing this content as "ammunition" to use, it is given as a series of pointers to the key issues that motivate Muslim 'belief', 'life', 'values', 'society' and 'culture'.

It's worth bearing in mind this list of five areas so we can regularly ask ourselves the question "How might this point of Islamic doctrine affect how my friend thinks about situation X?" As with committed Christians, we may (or may not) find a link between belief and practise. All too often what we believe does not always find expression in our behaviour.

To tease this out we will need to search our own heart and actions, as well as those of our Muslim friend. It also means using our eyes to watch as well as our mouths to engage with them in comparing notes on our experience of 'faith' and 'practise'. This begs the question: "How can we communicate with honesty and with a measure of trust?" and "How can we develop accurate enough 'communication' skills?" This is where we turn in the next chapter.

CHAPTER EIGHT

The Communication Barrier

Christians and Muslims use a different word to refer to the same thing and then the same word to refer to a different thing.

Steve Bell

I was in a town centre and a street-preacher was preaching. A small group gathered including a handful of young South Asian Muslim men. The preacher kept shouting "Jesus is the Son of God!" which agitated the young Muslims. He assumed everyone understood. So when the South Asians challenged him he simply said "It's the truth so just deal with it". Things got so heated they were about to pull him off his soap-box, so I asked the preacher to listen to what the young men were saying. When he was listening they accused him of saying that God had a physical relationship with Mary and Jesus was their son. The preacher said: "I didn't say that". So I said: "You may not have said it but by calling Jesus the 'Son of God' without explaining what it means, that is what these guys heard!" In fact some Muslims actually think that when Christians use the word "Trinity" they are referring to God the Father, Mary the mother and Jesus their baby. The Roman Catholic expression also seems to underline that mistaken idea for them.

I went on to explain to the young Muslims that it's possible to call someone who is never at home a "son of the street"; in a similar way Jesus is so closely identified with God that he is seen as the same thing and called the "son of God". It's not as a physical description (i.e. by pro-creation) but a 'spiritual title'. I knew what I had said had helped when one of them said: "Oh is that all Christians mean".

Well – no – that's not all that Christians mean. A lot more needs to be said on the matter but it is enough for a first encounter with this truth. At least it helped the young Muslims to keep open a category in their minds for the Holy Spirit to continue to work with which prepared them for the next Christian who would be able to build on this rudimentary start.[1]

The fourth barrier to developing a friendship between a Christian and a Muslim is successful communication. This is an 'art' rather than a 'science'. By that I mean it's a skill to be developed not a set of facts or theories to be learned. If we don't develop the skill the relationship is doomed from the start because – when we are left to our own devices – we tend to speak past someone from another culture without realising we are doing it.

We have seen already that both 'verbal' and 'non-verbal' forms of communication are equally important. Non-verbal communication includes things such as the way we dress; our attitude; how we do things; the tone with which we speak; and our body language. All these things say a lot about us to a Muslim, even before we open our mouths.

It's only when we have grasped this fundamental point that we are ready to think about the possible problems which can be caused by the words we say.

The Process of Communication

Many people think that communication is only about one thing – transmitting a message. Time and energy is put into sharpening and polishing that message. However, there is more to it than that. To communicate successfully we need to be aware of two other parts to what is a process rather than an event. So the three basic parts in the process are as follows:

1 transmit the message
2 how that message is understood
3 check that the message has been received in the intended way

If all three are done properly successful communication has taken place. However if the hearer understands the message to mean something different from what was originally intended, communication has not taken place. So just telling the gospel to a Muslim doesn't necessarily mean we have 'communicated' with them.

It comes as a shock to many Christians when they find out that many Christian terms and expressions they use actually carry quite a different meaning for a Muslim. Here are some examples of the communication barrier in action as Christians and Muslims misunderstand one another's words.

WORD	MUSLIM UNDERSTANDING
Acknowledgement - Aubrey Whitehouse 'Watch Your Language'	
God unknowable	distant, capricious, unpredictable,
Jesus Christ	prophet of Islam, never died, translated to heaven, will return to marry, have children and bring Islam to the world
Holy Spirit	the Angel Gabriel
Trinity	a polytheistic idol. Some Muslims think it is God the father, Mary the mother and Jesus their son
Bible	originally containing the word of God, now changed, and corrupted

WORD	MUSLIM UNDERSTANDING
sin	a mistake categorised in a hierarchy by God. *'God leads astray the evil doers and God does what He will'* (S4.52). Sin is to be improved upon next time, not inborn, not inevitable, there is no 'original sin'
faith	a mental assent to the articles of belief - *'No soul can believe except by the will of God'* (S10.99)
repentance	this is determined by God's initiative and control. *'God guides to Him all who are penitent* (S13.27-30), *'No choice have they (men)* (S28.67). Muslims might see their response to God's enabling as a stiffened resolve based on feeling sorry for getting caught
forgiveness	God decides to offer clemency, only known for certain on Judgement Day *'He punishes whom He pleases and has mercy on whom He pleases'* (S29.20)
guilt	the shame of being caught
redemption	the paying of compensation for a sin. There are seven mentions in the Qur'an. This only place where sacrifice occurs is Abraham sacrificing his son in S37.99-110 where Islamic tradition claims it is Ishmael (not Isaac) who is ransomed rather than Abraham. n.b. This is not linked to sin.
salvation	uncertain, obtained by belief and good works, God delivering you out of trouble like King David the psalmist
sanctification	outward performance and appearance, obedience to ceremonial ritual
love	tendency to think of the erotic in humans, conditional in God, "love" is not one of the 99 Names of God recognised in Islam.
heaven	male domain of sensuous and erotic pleasure.

WORD	MUSLIM UNDERSTANDING
hell	place of torment for those who find God's disapproval on Judgement Day
new birth	unheard of
grace	not understood, synonymous with mercy, God deciding to be kind
demons	the *jinn*, neutral spirit entities capable of good or evil, need appeasing sometimes by magical ocultic practices

Ideas for getting alongside a Muslim friend include the following:

- Ask God to develop his love in you for Muslims you know

- Introduce yourself and learn a greeting in their language

- Send sweets and a card on feast days

- Visit a friend in his/her home (don't invite to yours, they will reciprocate)

- Offer to pray when your friend has a problem (and do it)

- Develop a natural, agenda-free relationship

- Offer practical help e.g. baby-sit their children, teach English

- Be sensitive to points of 'felt-need' e.g. illness, infertility, demonic attack

- Become known to the senior male in the household

- Have 'spiritual' chats about the heart and what's going on inside

- Try to read the Bible one-on-one

- Hold international friendship evenings in your church

- Offer a multi-cultural kindergarten in your church

- Set up a 'Homework Club' or 'Language Café'

- Make friends on *Facebook* through your blog, *Instagram* or *Twitter* then meet up face-to-face

So we now know that – when we talk with someone from a Muslim background – we need to remember to choose our words as carefully as we can; then monitor the reaction as we speak and they respond; then do a final check to be clear what they actually think we have said.

A similar check needs to be done when a Muslim tells us something. It always helps to say "Just a minute, what I think you just said was…" and reflect back to them what you think you heard and let them correct you if it's inaccurate.

This is an essential tool in cross-cultural communicating in a 'plural society' where cultures mingle and rub-off on one another. And there are not many urban situations around the world where there is not some measure of multi-cultural society. So this is where we turn next and think about what it means to be a neighbour in the biblical sense in such 'plural' societies.

Sources:
1 *Gospel for Muslims – reading the Bible with eastern eyes,* by Steve Bell, Authentic Media, 2012

CHAPTER NINE

Neighbours in a Plural Society

Pluralism works as Jews for nothing marry Christians for nothing. They get on because they have everything in common - nothing.

Dennis Prager (Jewish author)

There is a tension in societies which have become multi-cultural. The presence of immigrants tends to instil a caution in the host population. It's all too easy to see new-comers as 'outsiders' – even when they've been resident for some generations. In recent years the 'migrant highway' has opened up in the wake of Islamist repression. This has provoked various reactions from compassion to resentment.

For some sections of a host-society may become 'politically correct' (i.e. over-tolerant) such as in northern Europe where 'anything less than total toleration will not be tolerated'. This is due to a sense of equal rights for all with no discrimination allowed on the basis of age, gender, race, religion or sexual orientation – a mantra of western values.

For other sections of the host-society immigration provokes racial tension (i.e. intolerance) and the flourishing of 'right-wing' politics and neo-Nazi vigilante groups which aim to defend host territory against perceived invasion.

It's ironic how some life-choices are tolerated such as smoking; drug dependency; divorce and family breakdown; and alternative sexual lifestyles, while Christians (and Muslims) are under pressure not to be judgemental about chaotic ethics and a 'morality of convenience'. In such liberal societies the notion of the 'uniqueness of Jesus Christ' is challenged. In fact the idea that a Christian has a "right" to share the gospel with someone from another faith community is now rejected – even by some Evangelicals. I am accused of being one of them because I champion a way of doing it that is 'non-standard' but which, I believe, is more culturally appropriate and less offensive to the politically correct notions about proselytism.

All this prompts the question: "Who is My Neighbour?" (Lk.10:29) which becomes even more critical in a plural society. Jesus' response to the question was to tell the parable of the Good Samaritan where it is the immigrant that is the "neighbour". The following list is the migration story of Britain which makes a helpful illustration of how far back the migration process can go in some host countries.

IMMIGRATION TO BRITAIN

700 B.C.	Celtic peoples arrived
43 A.D.	Romans arrived to occupy including soldiers from Gaul, Spain, Germany, Balkans, Asia Minor and even Africa

IMMIGRATION TO BRITAIN

400 A.D. — Saxons, Angles & Jutes from Europe began raiding the island

800 A.D. — Viking raids started from Scandinavia

1066 A.D. — invasion by William the Conqueror of Normandy

12th Century — Irish economic immigration to England

16th Century — Swarthy southern Europeans were thought to be spies for the Pope, the Jesuits or the King of Spain. Black Africans arrived in slavery

17th Century — Oliver Cromwell welcomed Jews back after expulsion by Edward 1 300 years earlier. They made London a financial capital of the world

Late 17th Century — Half a million Protestant French Huguenots brought weaving and silk working to Britain, fleeing persecution by King Louis XIV

18th Century — Thousands of Scots moved to England to seek their fortune after the Act of Union. Jewish immigration continued.

18th Century — Catholic French aristocrats (previously the persecutors of the Huguenots) fled to Britain to escape the French Revolution

Early 19th Century — A monkey survived the shipwreck of a French vessel. It was thought to be a Frenchmen and hung. Chinese seamen began arriving.

Late 19th Century — Arrivals from America and British colonies

Early 20th Century — Arrival of Jews while Eastern and southern Europeans received sanctuary in Britain during World War II and afterwards

Mid 20th Century — Arrival of economic migrants from the Caribbean and Asia helped build the British economy

IMMIGRATION TO BRITAIN

Late 20th Century   Arrival of migrants from the Muslim World, Africa and South East Asians have come on professional assignments, to spend money on medical treatment, as students, or as political asylum-seekers and refugees

Early 21st Century   Arrival of economic migrants from Europe as part of the EU; N.Africans, M.Eastern & W.Asians fleeing conflict or poverty

In the Gospel of Luke Jesus met a successful and upwardly mobile young man who had a hidden agenda. How could he manipulate Jesus into justifying his personal philosophy of life? The young man asks: "*What shall I do to inherit eternal life?*"(Lk.10:25). Jesus answers the question with the question: "*What is written in the Law? How do you understand it?*"(v26). Like many of us, the young man gives the answer he had grown up with: "*Love the LORD your God with all your heart, soul, strength and mind* (from Deut.6.5) *and love your neighbour as yourself*" (Lk.10:27; see also Lev.19:18). "*Correct*", says Jesus: "*Do this and live*" (Lk.10:28). He didn't co-operate with the agenda behind the question so the young man is forced to reveal more. He asks: "*And who is my neighbour?*" (v29). For him a 'neighbour' is someone of the same race, social class, income bracket and even choice in religion i.e. 'people like me'.

Racism can be understood as refusing another person who isn't 'in our own image'! This is what's going on in the parable of the Good Samaritan which Jesus went on to tell. It's a clear challenge to racism towards immigrants. The parable is actually teaching the Old Testament principle: '*The immigrant living amongst you in your land must be treated as one of your native born. Love him as yourself*. (Lev.19:33)

In the parable, an anonymous man is mugged. Like migrant Muslims today, Samaritans were a tolerated minority with a legal right of residence. Also, like Muslims, Samaritans practised a hybrid version of Judaism. A key point of the story is that it was the Samaritan who '*did justly, loved mercy and walked humbly with God*' (Mic.6:8), while the priest and the Levite were full of racial and religious superiority – but failed by passing by the anonymous mugged man because they didn't recognise him as a 'neighbour' (Lk.10:31-33).

After telling the parable Jesus moves in for the punch-line saying:

"*Which was the neighbour to the man in need?*" (Lk.10:36). "*He who showed mercy*" says the young man. Jesus concludes "*You go and do the same*" (v37). How can we do the same? Who is the 'neighbour' for me today? I can't help everyone! How do I choose? What does God want me to do? As individuals we can best start by responding to those around us on a daily basis. A local church can also respond in four 'neighbourhood' spheres...

1 Jerusalem (locally) - mono-culturally

2 Judea (regionally & nationally) - mono & bi-culturally

3 Samaria (adjacent nations continentally) - bi-culturally

4 to the ends of the earth (globally) - cross-culturally

The very view of reality that gives rise to the beliefs and practices of ordinary Muslims is in many respects closer to the biblical one than to the missionary's own mechanistic, scientific world view.

Rt. Rev. Dr Bill Musk, former bishop in Tunis

The apostle Paul is clear: '*The love of Christ constrains us...*' (2 Cor.5:14) i.e. it hems us in like the banks of a great river that's flowing out of the heart of God. His heart expressed through us, leads us out of our 'Jerusalem' into the world of need among all races cultures and faiths i.e. the poor, the widows, the fatherless, the oppressed, the needy, the disenfranchised and the sexually abused and confused; all of which are an issue in immigrant and host communities.

As Christians we are not an end in ourselves but we are God's means to a greater end – i.e. to be a blessing to those who are not-yet-churched among all nations (Rom.15). In the New Testament understanding of mission, we exist for our neighbours in the 'regions beyond'. I am encouraged by St. Paul's Assemblies of God Church in Worcester, where there is a sign over the exit of the building saying - 'The ends of the earth start here!'. This is a clear statement of a New Testament understanding of the missionary nature of the church.

The hidden world of Muslim Women

Christian approaches to Muslims have traditionally focussed on the men but a lesser understood aspect is the significance of Muslim women. Some argue that it's the Muslima (female Muslim) who is key to the Muslim community; this is because it's the women who maintain family; provide social continuity; uphold the values of religion in the home; shape of the worldview of their children and nurture of the culture. These days, due to war and migration, more women are actually head of a household. Yet the way women experience Islam is quite different to men. The reason includes the issues such as the following:

- Traditional 'patriarchal' social patterns dictate that a woman manages the interior world of the home while a man manages the exterior world beyond the home

- Females are custodians of a household's moral honour so they are 'protected' and therefore somewhat sheltered by the males of the family and are not free to move around or make choices as males are allowed to do

- Males are circumcised on the eighth day (as in the Bible) but in some Islamically dominated cultures, pre-Islamic practices persist such as girls being subject to female circumcision (i.e. genital mutilation); other rituals can follow on marriage, or when pregnant, or on delivery of a child

- Due to the female menstrual cycle there can also be rituals linked to ceremonial purity, as found in the Old Testament Torah

- Women can be segregated to pray in certain parts of a mosque, which has led some women to set up all-female piety movements

Women are to the 'house of Islam' what the wind-sock is to an airfield. They show which way the proverbial wind is blowing; politically, religiously and socially.

In the old days:

At the start of Islam men and women were moral equals in the sight of God and early Islam generally improved the status of women, compared to earlier Arab cultures. It prohibited female infanticide; recognized women's personhood; made marriage contractual requiring a dowry to the woman, rather than to her family; guaranteed the legal right of females to own and manage property; introduced the right to receivefinancial maintenance in marriage, after divorce and when widowed.

Historic records assert Muhammad consulted and included women; and appointed at least one female Imam. Women contributed to the canonization of the Quran; took part in the transmission of *hadith* and did editorial correction on the written ruling on dowry by a Caliph. Women prayed in mosques without segregation from men; engaged in business and even held political power.

Islam has credentials that challenge some Christian understanding of gender roles. However, the status of women in contemporary Muslim societies no longer conforms to any Qur'anic ideal but is informed by the prevailing patriarchal cultural norms. As a result improvement in the status of women has become a major issue among Muslims. Since the mid-nineteenth century, men and women have questioned the legal and social restrictions on women, especially regarding education, seclusion, strict veiling, polygamy, slavery, and having concubines.

Progressive Muslims see women and gender issues as crucial to social development. Debates continue today over the appropriate level of female participation in the public sphere. Tensions remain between traditionalists, who advocate continued patriarchy, and liberal democracies which support progressive Muslim advocates who press for the continued liberation of women.[1]

Natural ways to meet Muslims
Natural friendship with both female and male Muslims is the goal of our interaction with a Muslim. Here are some ideas about where we are likely to see this happen.

- By using their business services

- In the work place

- Making a point of greeting them in the street (Mat.5:47)

- Christian community projects – vocational training, English teaching etc

- Joint Christian/Muslim community service projects or sporting events

- Social Media - making friends on *Facebook*, through your blog and following on *Instagram* or *Twitter*

- Door-to-door
  Though less natural and impersonal, door-to-door can be a useful way of first contact when accompanied by the Jesus Film DVD or a questionnaire. On a feast day it can be acceptable to Muslims if

we visit them and make a gift of Gospel (or a Scripture portion) in their heart-language and with Islamic cover design. This is because the Gospel (Injil) is one of their holy books.

- Telling your own story
  When speaking about spiritual things with people from Muslim backgrounds it always helps to remember that eastern cultures use picture-language in the way western cultures use proverbs. For instance when talking about why people do sinful things we can explain the biblical teaching about 'original sin' by using the expression Adam sinned in the garden of Eden and 'like father like son' we are children of Adam and so we are sinners like him.

If a Muslim has English as a second or third language, it's helpful to use simple expressions. Don't speak of personal relationship with God but acceptance by him and his answers to prayer and activity in your experience. Do speak about the joy of personal prayer that comes from the heart, rather than rote learned or what are you are required to say; speak also of the fact that God answers. To do this, try to use the Bible and encourage a Muslim friend to use the Qur'an (if they can) to back-up what they say. Remember you are a "Believer in Jesus" and always speak about him clearly and simply. Don't bother talking about your church, denomination; not Christianity in general but Christ.

- Greetings cards
  On special occasions, send greeting cards in their heart-language (n.b. available from CPO – see Appendix 3).

- Videos
  Story telling is part of many Muslim cultures so videos are an effective and attractive medium to them. There is good material available in English and vernacular Languages (see Appendix 3). The Jesus Film is one of the most widely used, though this is best placed with Muslims who are already showing interest in the gospel. A follow-up questionnaire and Bible study to accompany the Jesus Film, is also available in English on YouTube.

- Special events at a local church
  It's best to use events which include the family, such as Christmas; Father's Day; Mother's Day or Harvest Thanksgiving. Where possible it's better to include their national music and/or simple songs or psalms in vernacular languages, drama and dance with a short message, which emphasises story telling. Plenty of time is needed afterwards

for eating. Appropriate Christian literature can be made available in their vernacular languages. People who welcome guests at the door, should be gender appropriate; i.e. men dealing with men and women with women.

Following Jesus in a liberal democracy now means engaging in a 'counter-cultural' activity – namely to intentionally reach-out to Muslims with the hope they will follow Jesus with us. This doesn't make 'friendship' a ruse or a deception but a courtesy. Christian life and witness in a plural society is not a 'right' but a 'responsibility'. By engaging in this obligation we are standing on the shoulders of the believers in Jesus who have gone before who said 'We must obey God rather than men.' (Acts 5:29)

So how do we actually engage a Muslim friend with the good news about Jesus? What should we do? What should we not do? This is where we go next.

Sources:
1 http://www.oxfordislamicstudies.com/article/opr/t125/e2510

CHAPTER TEN

Discussing the Good News with a Muslim Friend

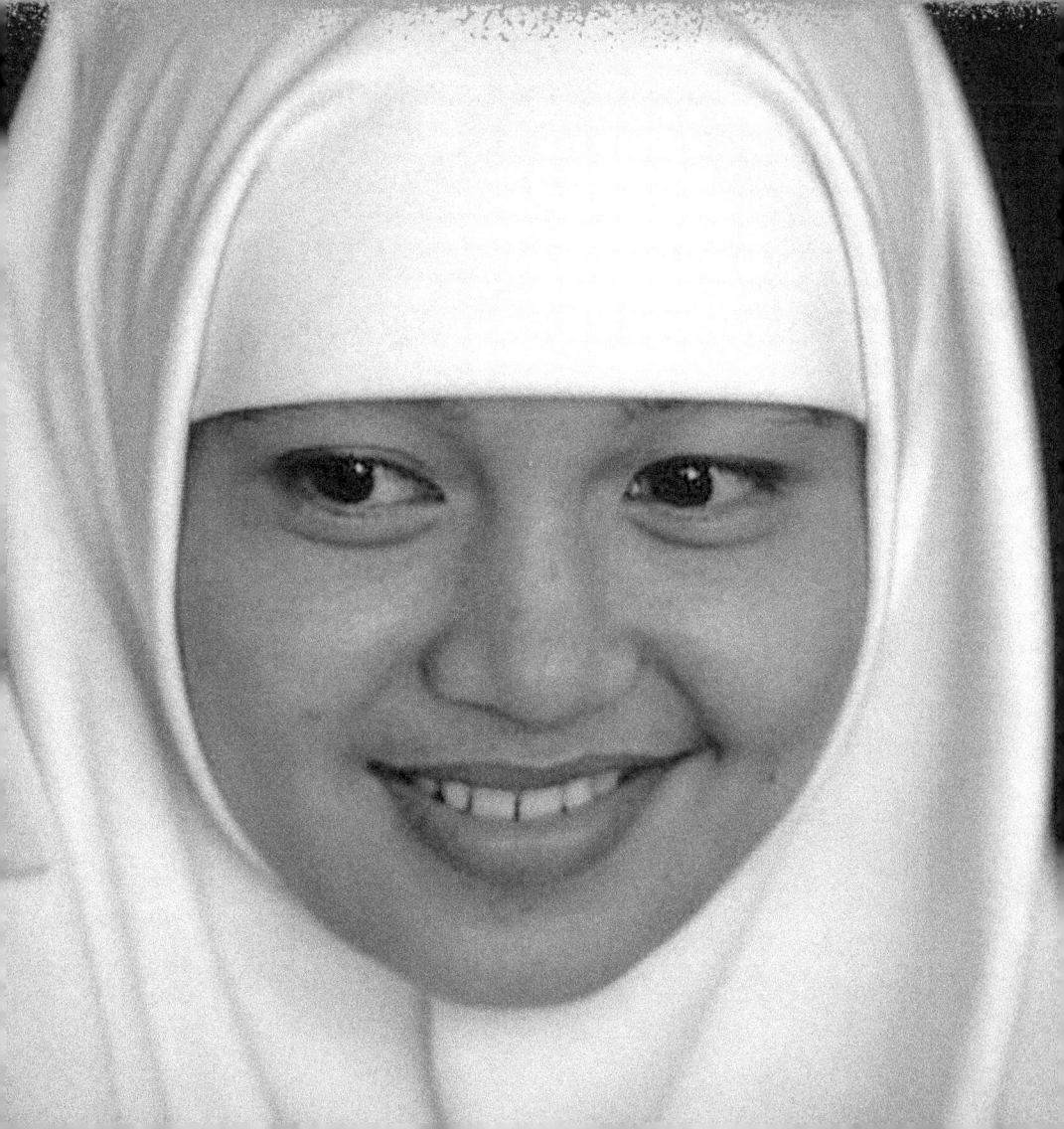

Muslims need to be met within the context of Islam. The spiritual revolution must occur from within his own socio-cultural context. We must carry the living Christ with all his power to heal, exorcise and save into the real world of ordinary Muslims, and trust him to meet heart hunger without implicit condemnation of their cultural heritage. Can Christ trust us that much?

Rt. Rev. Dr. Bill Musk, former bishop in Tunis

What has been said so far is a preparation for the question: "How can I discuss the Good News with a Muslim friend?" The answer begins with the fact that the key word is "friend". Until you can see a particular person with a Muslim background as a 'friend' (or someone you want to try to befriend) you will find it more difficult to get the place of trust where the time is right to discuss the good news about Jesus with them. This ground work involves investing in the befriending process because achieving friendship is like laying a foundation. It's time-consuming and there's no quick-fix, as the Apostle Paul made clear; it's a matter of a lifestyle and a process:

'Therefore, since through God's mercy we have this ministry...we don't use deception, nor do we distort the word of God... by setting forth the truth plainly we commend ourselves to everyone's conscience in the sight of God.' (2 Cor.4:1-2)

This is partly why Christians are easily tempted to ignore the issue all together opting only to "witness" to them or give them some literature and walk away. That's an important and useful thing to do but on its own it's only half the job done. As a prelude to discipleship, a relationship of trust (i.e. friendship) seems to be the non-negotiable key context to establish.

I find that some Muslims and Christians remain sceptical that it's even possible to arrive at 'friendship' and so abandon the idea. My response is that there's one good reason why it is possible and we should try – namely because Islamic teaching points in that direction when it encourages a Muslim to relate to non-Muslims *'with respect'* (S16.125) and in the *'best possible way'* (S29.46), even to *'make friends of enemies'* (S41.34).

As we gain the trust of a Muslim friend, we are able to discuss spiritual issues. The more trust is developed, the more right we have to speak.

But whatever rules people wish to lay down about how to engage in 'cross-cultural communication' the next person you talk to may well break the rule. For example just this week I greeted a newly engaged couple from Muslim family backgrounds, who were actually cuddling each other in public (away from the Muslim community I should add). In the same way every Muslim is different, despite some important common aspects. So when trying to move from a viable human friendship into a 'spiritual friendship' the same applies.

So here are some commonalities that I have found helpful when taking the conversation further:

- Use your personal story (see 1 Thess.2:8)

- Be content to explain the Good News, one aspect at a time

- Use picture language rather than abstract or theoretical language (Mat.13:3)

- Use illustrations – articles, blogs or books can often get an idea over better than discussion e.g. for a younger Muslim, the film *Les Miserables* by Victor Hugo is a powerful study of grace.

- Encourage your friend to read the Gospels for themselves, preferably not Mark as this begins '*This is the gospel of Jesus Christ the Son of God*'(Mk.1:1).

- Try to help your friend understand the reasons *why* the gospel is needed i.e. our inability to help ourselves and that we are in need of the 'lift of grace'.

- Try to address 'heart-hunger' rather than doctrinal argument.

- Ask for the space to explain the gospel fully, uninterrupted, before discussing.

Dialogue is the serious address and response between two persons, in which the being and truth of each is confronted by the being and truth of the other. It involves relationship and words and seeks to know life through the other person.

Reuel Howe

Proclamatory dialogue

When we have established sufficient connection and conversation is ready to go a little deeper. Proclamatory dialogue is the outcome. It simply means to 'proclaim' the good news in an atmosphere of 'dialogue' rather than monologue. This is an important part of the 'grace and truth' approach to friendship is to try to put yourself into the shoes of a Muslim. It's possible to ask questions which – rather than challenging or condemning them – can affirm them as an individual seeker after God and help them feel comfortable enough to answer more honestly. For example if we ask: "How does it feel to fast and what spiritual benefit do you feel?" it opens conversation; builds the bridge and encourages a friend to come out onto it to meet us in the middle. As trust grows, we earn the right to go deeper. This is the essence of 'Proclamatory Dialogue', which is a helpful tool, whereby we dialogue while proclaiming good news (see Appendix 2). One of the first steps is to try to use social greetings in the vernacular language of your friend. Here are some ideas.

Some basic Muslim phrases:

Arabic:

marhaba!	hello (informal non-religious)
asslaamu alaikum	peace on you (used for "hello" and "goodbye", like the Hebrew shalom alekhem)
wi alaikum assalaam	and peace on you too (response to the above)
al hamdu lillah	Praise God (expression of thankfulness)
ma assalaama	goodbye
eid al-mubarak	Happy feast day
Ramadan ikareem	Happy Ramadan

Urdu & Persian:

Suber khair	good morning

Next it helps to have some idea about how to open a conversation so here are some ideas for that too.

Culture & language – what about his/her family place of origin, their customs and language? (I.E. Related to birth, weaning of infants, coming of age, courtship, marriage, death).

Feast days – what is the significance for them of a recent or forthcoming feast?

Prayer – what does it mean for their relationship "to" god? Explain the contrast with the christian offer of a relationship "with" god through jesus christ? Does your friend pray prayers of *du'a* (personal petition in their own words) in addition to salat (*prescribed*) prayer? If god is almighty and everything comes as 'fate' from his decrees, what is the purpose of prayer at all?

The islamic creed – *'there is no god but god and muhammed is the apostle of god'*. What does it mean to them?

Fasting – ask about the feast of ramadan. What is their personal experience of it and what spiritual benefits come from it for them personally? (Is.58).

Amulets – (i.E. Charms to ward off evil) what do they mean?; How do they protect from dark powers? Do they think god prefers his word to be around our necks or in our hearts – why? (Ps.119:11)

Islamism – how does your friend feel about islamist attacks and why?

The veil – why? And when? Do they wear the veil (*hijab or burqa*)? Why do they think christian women do not wear a veil? (Is.61:10; Rom.13:14)

Halal foods – what does your friend think about its significance? Where do they buy these food stuffs?

Almsgiving – compare muslim and christian ways of giving. (2 Cor.9:6-15)

Pilgrimage – what is the significance of pilgrimage in islam? Have they been to mecca and what meaning did it have for them? (Jn.14:1-6)

Forgiveness – what does this mean in islam? How does your muslim friend feel about waiting for judgement day? Has your friend ever asked for forgiveness and received it? How did they know they had been forgiven?

Fear – what does your friend fear most - death, hell, sickness, demon possession, loss of face and why?

Crisis – what does your muslim friend do in a crisis – do they go to a friend? To family? To an imam? To a magical practitioner? To other? (See ps.121)

Salvation history – trace some key qur'anic figures (e.G. Adam, abraham, moses & jesus). What is their significance for your muslim friend?

Scripture – what does your friend think about the bible and the qur'an? (Gen.22: Ex.12; Num.19:9; Jn.3:14; 10:12, 24; Rom.6:23; Eph.2:8; 1 Tim.2:4-5; Heb.9:22; 10:1-8,12)

The news – what does your friend think about current affairs such as the migrant crisis; the behaviour of islamists; the concern of progressive muslims to see reform.

We also find the principle of 'proclamatory dialogue' in Jesus' ministry. Even as a boy, the Lord modelled it. Notice how he genuinely listened while humbly having something to say. Observe him doing five things in his discourse with the elders in the Temple in Luke 2:45-46.

1 sitting among the teachers
2 listening
3 asking questions
4 gaining and exhibiting understanding
5 giving answers to questions asked of him

This is a pattern for us to follow with our Muslim friend. Remember that we are only one link in the chain of God's dealings with them. They may even be further on than we think, which was the case with Cornelius just before he met the apostle

The gift of the gospel must come wrapped in you!

Peter in Acts10:1-6. God was aware of Cornelius' prayers even before he had heard the Good News from Peter and had the chance to believe. This might also tell us something about God's dealings with Muslims, even before they believe in Jesus? For some Muslim believers in Jesus, it's a process of divine activity in their lives rather than a crisis intervention, which brings them to faith in Christ.

Handling controversy

It's only natural to be defensive about things we care about so we need to listen to our friend's heart and try to speak in ways that open up conversation rather than shut it down. Controversial questions that will shut down a conversation if we let them include: Has the Bible been changed?; Do Christians worship three gods?; Was Jesus the biological offspring of a sexual union between God and Mary?; Did Jesus die on the Cross?; Is the West intrinsically Christian?; Do all Christians support the political State of Israel?; Do all Christians drink alcohol and eat pork – why?. So resist the temptation to quarrel (2 Tim.2:23-26). It helps to criticise 'Islamism' rather than Islam *per se* as this helps to keep the conversation open because there are biblical tenets in Islam that can point to Christ (Mat.7:1-5).

- Work at removing misunderstanding by asking why your Muslim friend thinks as he or she does.

- Always try to distinguish between what are essential and non-essential, central and peripheral, primary and secondary issues, within Christian and Islamic belief. This helps us not to deviate into unhelpful cul-de-sacs.

- Be prepared to admit and even ask forgiveness for any violations committed against Muslims by Christians in the past and present (Ps.106:6; Rom.2:24).

- Take every opportunity to say what you believe and why you believe it (1 Pet.3:15).

- The aim is not to win an argument but to win the person. It's possible to lose the argument and still win the person, if love is our orientation.

- Be patient. Muslim people take time to assimilate and respond to new truth, just as we do.

So these are just some practical pointers to help us get started in actually moving a personal friendship on towards becoming a 'spiritual friendship'. That can only happen by intentionally interacting with someone from a Muslim background. But remember, it's an 'art' not a 'science' because everyone – Muslim or Christian – brings such different variables to a conversation.

Having said that it's an exciting time to be engaging affably with Muslims about spiritual issues at a time when people from Muslim backgrounds are changing allegiance to follow Jesus in significant numbers. We need to come to terms with this reality which is why it's the focus of the next chapter.

CHAPTER ELEVEN

How some Muslims are Finding Christ

Perhaps it is time to stop expecting the Muslim to see the love of God in the cross of Christ. It might be easier for him to glimpse there something of Christ's loyalty to his Father, something of the Father's glory in watching his Son obey him to the end, vindicating family honour.

Rt. Rev. Dr. Bill Musk, former bishop in Tunis

According to research by Dr David Garrison[1] Muslims are changing their faith allegiance to Jesus Christ now more than at any time in church history. In fact there have been more Muslim 'people movements' to Christ in the past fourteen years than the last fourteen centuries – a 'people movement' is defined as either 1,000 people coming to Christ from a Muslim background, or else 100 worshipping communities are established among such people.

God is clearly at work among Muslims but while this is encouraging we need to remember that these developments are like a pin-prick on an elephant's back. We also need to be aware that these new believers are becoming followers of Christ not institutional Christianity.

In my book *Gospel for Muslims* I stress that the Bible doesn't require anyone to use the term "Christian". This may be appropriate for those of us from 'culturally-Christian' societies but it can create unnecessary misunderstanding in Muslim communities where the term suggests that a member of the community has abandoned their family heritage. The other problem with the term "Christian" is that it's a politically loaded term due to its association with the Crusades and Empire and western domination in the world.

But how are so many Muslims turning to Jesus? In my experience there are four main ways (or a mixture of them) in which Muslims most frequently turn to Christ. These are as follows...
- Reading the Bible with an open mind
- Knowing a Christian over a period of time
- Sincere comparison and search through the Qur'an to the Bible
- Supernatural intervention of God

A survey, which bears this out, was conducted by Dr Dudley Woodberry conducted a survey, which bears this out.[2] Around 600 believers in Jesus from a Muslim background were questioned and they spoke of the reasons why they left the religious component of Muslim culture to follow Jesus in spite of the potential persecution, hardship and death threats.

'Farida is from a Muslim family. She became a Christian in the summer of 2001 during an outreach at the chapel of a Christian hospital where she had received loving treatment by medical staff. There was concern about Farida's nurture in Christ because she is illiterate. She was urged to listen to Christian radio. One evening she found her elder brother listening to the same broadcast and discovered that he too had become a Christian while working on a farm where he had made friends with a Christian. Farida's brother is educated and reads the Scripture to her, which encourages her.'

The study found the following reasons…

1 The certainty of salvation in Christ compared to the uncertainty of the Islamic tradition, which says that the bridge to heaven is only as wide as a human hair. Not even good deeds can guarantee a safe crossing. According to Islamic teaching, even the prophet Muhammad does not know if he will make it to heaven.

2 The character and teaching of Christ is attractive – his humility, non-retaliation and love for the weak and marginalised.

3 The character of Christians – their work for justice and 'mercy ministry' to the needy – including Muslims – their tranquility and inner peace.

4 Over 25% have had some sort of supernatural intervention by dreams, visions of angels and/or Jesus, healings and miraculous occurrences. Jesus has even spoken to them and announced the healing of a loved-one which then happens.

An Egyptian man was reading Luke's Gospel and reached chapter 3 when a strong wind entered the room and a voice said: "I am Jesus Christ whom you hate. I am the Lord you are seeking". The man said: "I cried and cried and decided to follow Jesus".

An Afghan man was imprisoned by the Taliban. Having nothing to do in jail he started reading a dictionary and his eyes fell on the word "Jesus". Every time he read it a supernatural presence filled the cell. This triggered his search for the meaning of the word and his conversion. He is now a fearless evangelist within Afghanistan.
(Friday Fax 2001)

A Muslim's Story:
'I have always felt attracted to Islam. I memorised the Qur'an at the age of six. I was certain Islam was the religion of truth and Christianity the religion of blasphemy. I avoided the Bible thinking it was a distorted book.
The first time I saw a Bible was at college where began to spend every spare minute studying it alongside the Qur'an, determined to prove the Bible wrong.
    Soon doubts about the Qur'an crept into my mind. I came across

John 3:16 and that night I dreamt I heard a voice repeating this verse over and over. The dream kept recurring so the following morning I went to the friend who gave me the Bible. He told me God was speaking to me. I challenged him: 'If I hear the voice again I'll be a Christian with you. If I don't then you have to become a Muslim with me'.

That night I heard the voice again three times so I accepted Jesus Christ as Lord and Saviour of my life. I was expelled by my family and thrown out of college but with Open Doors' help I studied in a Bible school abroad.' (Source: Open Doors)

Without being triumphalist about it, we can celebrate the fact that multiplied thousands of Muslims are changing allegiance to Jesus. Our role is to be a winsome encourager and friend to those we know who are on this journey or about to set out on the journey to Christ. We need to see ourselves more as 'spiritual midwives' than over-zealous evangelists. We are there to walk alongside; to assist; to inform; to discuss; to encourage; to pray; to love; and to support as a 'spiritual friend', rather than a combative critic. As such people from Muslim family backgrounds are coming to faith in Christ the need for 'mentoring' arises; this is simply another word for "discipling". The need to receive them into the appropriate fellowship of believers comes into the frame[3] along with the ongoing need to provide appropriate and culturally appropriate spiritual nurture for them from the Bible[4]. A brief introduction to both these aspects is the subject of the next chapter.

Sources:
1 Dr David Garrison, *A Wind in the House of Islam*, WIGTake Resources, 2014
2 J. Dudley Woodberry, Russell G. Shubin, and G. Marks, Why *Muslims Follow Jesus*, October 24, 2000
3 T. Green & Roxy, *Joining the Family*, Kitab Interserve Resources, 2016
4 T. Green, *Come Follow Me*, www.lulu.com, 2013

CHAPTER TWELVE

Mentoring Believers from Islam

A close-knit Muslim community is an entrenched cultural web enmeshing people in deep loyalty to the system. The underlying adherence to customs, community and family make individual decisions for Christ well-nigh impossible without fatally injuring those relationships.

Patrick Johnstone

I met a young woman from a conservative Islamic nation who told me her story. She was taken to the Gulf by her family to enter a forced marriage to a man within her own ethnic group who was working there. She soon had a child but then changed her faith-allegiance to Jesus.

Her husband reacted violently throwing her out of the home before divorcing her. Her family threatened to kill her so she fled as a refugee to Europe where one Sunday she passed a church with a glass front. She could see 'happy people' inside so she went in and asked them to help her.

The church took her in, along with her child and they became a new adoptive daughter and grand-daughter to a middle-aged couple in the church. The young woman is now a radiant and firm believer in Jesus. She is to be baptised along with her fiancé; a young man from her own ethnic group who was born and raised in the new country and is also a believer from a Muslim family.

This is how the local church can respond effectively and strategically to such opportunities with new believers from Muslim background. But what is a "believer of Muslim background" and how can we prepare ourselves to help them?

'Converts' or 'Proselytes'?

We need to be clear what we mean by "conversion" from Islam to Christ.

This *should* mean ...
...an individual repents, trusts Christ and undergoes a change of heart-allegiance from the religious aspect of Muslim culture, to Christ, while remaining in the Muslim community as a witness to them. (Acts 20:21)

This should *not* mean...
...an individual trusts Christ, joins a church and withdraws from their Muslim community and cultural roots.

The Bible affirms the first meaning and never mentions the second. When a new believer in Jesus from a Muslim family withdraws from his or her culture it's self-defeating because it's more likely to provoke unnecessary ostracism. In the past, such new believers were encouraged to leave their culture behind, even changing their birth-name (such as Ahmad) to a, so-called, 'Christian' name (such as 'Peter'). Today second and third generation believers from a Muslim background are bi-cultural because they have a western background. It's wrong to expect anyone to try to abandon their 'dual heritage'.

To do this is called 'extraction evangelism' and is the opposite of the Lord Jesus who would say: *'Go home and tell...'*. (Mat.11:4; Lk.7:22; 8:39;

Mk.5:19; 8:26).

Another important point is that although Jews are a unique category, for people born a Jew, Judaism is both an ethnicity and a religion. So when a Jewish person turns to Christ she remains ethnically Jewish while spiritually becoming a follower of Jesus. This makes her a Jewish believer in Jesus. In the same way a Pakistani from a Muslim family who comes to Christ is still ethnically and culturally Pakistani but simply becomes a Pakistani follower of Jesus of a Muslim background.

We need to remember that the gospel redeems us from the negative aspects of our birth culture, while enriching the aspects of it that are biblically affirmed. So rather than people withdrawing from their community and culture after conversion, it's vital that they become active among their own people during the period in which they are most effective as a fresh witness to Jesus.

The new believer from a Muslim family will be guided by God in negotiating the good and bad in their own culture, just as we are in ours. The Holy Spirit teaches which aspects of culture needs 'redeeming' and which aspects are affirmed by the Bible. Ultimately it's not us but God who shows these new believers how to be authentic witness to Jesus in their own community and culture. We must pray, support and trust God.

If we try to coerce the new believer of Muslim background into adopting aspects of the host culture or even to coerce them into becoming 'more cultural' in order to follow Jesus in the host culture, we have strayed into 'proselytism'. This sort of 'cultural transfer' was expected in the early church when Gentile proselytes adopted Jewish culture in addition to believing in the God of the Jews.

The early apostles adopted an 'integration' model and Paul in particular became angry over this very issue when he found proselytism going on; for example the Galatian church. However, the New Testament churches, non-Jewish believers were free to attach themselves to the church in their own way. Gentile believers joined the predominantly Jewish church while retaining an identity that was ethnically and culturally Greek – including their name and relational network (see Mk.5:1-20). As a result the Good News spread and the apostolic conclusion on the matter was as follows...

'It seemed good to us and to the Holy Spirit not to lay a greater burden on you other than that you abstain from consuming blood or the meat of strangled animals, and from sexual immorality.' (Acts 15:28-29)

Mentoring believers from Muslim backgrounds

Conversion:

Conversion for a Muslim as with anyone else is usually a mixture of 'crisis' and 'process'. Sometimes there are several crises along the way. The 'process' can be seen in the rational search of a Nicodemus (John 3) in contrast with the 'crisis' on the Damascus Road for Saul of Tarsus (Acts 9). Both are valid, which tells us that the discipling of believers of Muslim backgrounds usually starts *before* their heart-allegiance moves from Islam to Jesus Christ. Care is needed here though in order to keep clear in our minds that a Muslim who changes allegiance to Jesus, does not become a 'Christian' per se. This is because it has a negative historical and political overtone. The Muslim becomes a 'believer', a 'disciple' or a 'follower' of Jesus.

Persecution:

Persecution is not inevitable when Muslims follow Christ especially if they are from an open-minded or educated family. However in conservative and less educated households violent reaction is more likely.

Suffice it to say that Muslims who change allegiance to Jesus will likely face some form reaction from family or community – or both. The opposition can be on a spectrum from harmless antagonism, to actual ejection from the home to outright persecution or even death. This will likely come from their extended family and community. We need to think this through but not be deterred by it. It can help to have a grasp of why persecution occurs. It's driven by the cultural instinct to dispel the 'shame' the conversion imposes on the family or community – or both. To 'punish' the person bringing the 'shame', is a mechanism of expelling or deflecting it onto that person and away from those around them. It's also an attempt to protect the bringer of 'shame' from violating the social rules.

The basis for this opposition is the Qur'an's statement that anyone leaving Islam is committing 'apostasy' and is therefore a blasphemer, worthy of death by a relative upon whom the shame has been brought (S2.217; 3.90; 4.89;16.106-107). Each new believer's experience is different depending on their circumstances.

- Less educated and less 'world-aware' Muslim families are likely to have the stronger reaction, but this too is not always the case.

- It's ideal when the whole family or community converts, but this is rarely the case.

- Due to the honour/shame code prominent families are often more reactionary about the humiliation when family members leave Islam.

Ali burnt some people and this news reached Ibn Abbas, who said: 'Had I been in his place I would not have burnt them... [however] I would have killed them for the Prophet said: "If somebody (a Muslim) discards his religion, kill him".

Hadith Vol 4:52, 'Fighting for Allah's Cause' Ch 149 No.260 (pg 160-161)

It's good to know the Bible is no stranger to suffering and persecution. Here are some references, which may help – Mat.10:24-25; Acts 5:40-42; 1 Pet.4:12-16; Hebs.13:10-14. The tragic stories of persecution of believers from Muslim background, when it does happen, suggests to us that local churches need to be able to identify 'safe-houses' where endangered believers of a Muslim background can be placed for their safety.

A Muslim's story

'When my family found out about my conversion they felt disgraced. Putting me in an asylum would only bring more shame so they asked a Sheikh to talk to me. I prayed silently "Lord...please deliver me!" At the end the Sheikh said to my father "Sir, your son is alright. It is you who needs healing". My father beat me but I felt no pain. The family cut me off and refusing even to eat with me.

After seeing me come out of church my father was so angry he tore my clothes and threw me out of the house. Since then I have been moving from place to place knowing that my new family is the family of God"...

A Muslim young man from the south of Egypt

'Secret Believing':

If opposition occurs, it can be safer to take fellowship to the Muslim believer and not expect them to come to fellowship. Secret believers may feel the need to conceal their faith totally or at least in certain situations, for a period of time. They may be in physical danger of reprisals or else they are not ready (or willing) to lose their position in the family structure i.e. perhaps as recipient to a legacy or assured employment in an extended family business.

'Secret believers' are found in the Bible. Old Testament examples include Esther 2:8-11; 4:12-14; 7:3,4); Elijah in 1 Kgs.17:1-6 (see also 19:1-9); Naaman (2 Kgs.5:17-19). Then New Testament examples include Jn.3:1-10; 7:12-13, 50-52; 12:42-43; 19:38-42. This is not to suggest that "confession" of faith is not important; it's ultimately vital – see Mat.10:32-33 and Rom.10:9-10. However, we have to decide where the balance lies in the knowledge that it's our friend from a Muslim family that bears the brunt of the 'when'; 'how' and 'to whom' that confession happens. For us it can remain theoretical but to them it can be a matter of peace or hostility; ease or suffering; and even life or death.

There are differing opinions about what "confessing" Christ means (Rom.10:9,10). Paul did not specify who we confess to. It could be to God, to oneself or to family or friends. It follows that there are different levels of secrecy being practised by Muslims who could be in mortal danger if they 'confessed' to the wrong person. Secret believers vary – for example they may only confess to God; sometimes only one other person knows; sometimes only a support group of reliable Christian friends know or even a member of their family might know. In some cases everyone but the family or Muslim community know because the believer has moved location in order to be an open believer.

Only God knows the best time to 'go public' in the family network as this can do more harm than good in terms of hardening of the attitudes of others unnecessarily. The new believer needs to be supported as he or she prays about when the time is right. Ultimately it must be the decision of the new believer themselves as to when to make their allegiance to Jesus known.

Discipleship:

This can sound a cold and metallic kind of word but a 'disciple' is a *learner* or *student*. So discipleship is simply a relationship between a mentor and mentored. Having said that it is normally a 1-on-1 activity but Jesus mentored groups of 3, 12 and 70.

The first letter of the apostle John says: '*Our fellowship is with the Father and the Son… so you may have fellowship with us*' (1Jn.1:3) There is therefore a corporate aspect to discipleship and an ongoing time-frame. We are talking about 'whole-life' discipleship in the sense that it influences every area of our lives and for as long as we live. It can be helpful for a new believer from a Muslim background to develop several Christian friends to learn from. Such new believers are also likely to instinctively respond to the Bible with a Semitic mind-set which can enrich their Christian mentor; for example they bring a stronger grasp of God's holiness and living out systematic spiritual disciplines. They also accept more readily than westerners, the supernatural aspects such as dreams, visions and angels appearing.

The core activity of discipleship is teaching, so we need to re-examine...

- exactly what Jesus instructs us to teach. (see Mat.28:18-20)

- what the early church understood by 'discipling' of newer believers (Acts 2:42; 18:11, 25-26; 19:9-10; Hebs.6:1-2; 1 Pet.2:1-3, 4-5,9)

- the difference between biblical Christianity and western culture.

- what Paul meant when he urged Timothy to '*rebuke, correct and train in righteousness*'. (2 Tim.3:16).

- decide which of the Five Pillars a new believer from Islam should be expected to stop observing n.b. Paul still observed certain Jewish rites for specific reasons. What do you think they might have been?
  a) circumcision - Acts 16:1-3 (see also Acts 15:1-35; Gal.5:2-6)
  b) a Nazarite Vow - Acts 18:18 (see also Num.6:18)
  c) ritual purification - Acts 21:17-26

Popular Muslim opinion:

1 You cannot know God

2 Jesus was just a man

3 Jesus did not die on the Cross

4 The Bible is unreliable

Enquirers:

Topics to include in discussion with enquirers include...
- The Oneness of God
- God has made man in His own image
- God has given His laws
- God judges man for disobeying His laws
- God told His prophets that He would come among them
- The Person & work of Jesus

- The disciples recognised Jesus as Messiah
- The Jews killed Jesus
- God raised Jesus from the dead
- God gives the Holy Spirit to believers in Jesus

(Acknowledgement - Vivienne Stacey - practical lessons for Evangelism among Muslims, 1988)

New believers:

Topics to include in discussion with new believers...
- Salvation - repentance, faith, baptism in water & Spirit
- Submission & obedience to Christ
- Spiritual disciplines - prayer, bible study, worship, praise, fasting, giving, meditation
- Breaking of bread
- Fellowship
- Healing
- Relationship with God, Christians, other Muslims & family
- Holiness of life
- Witness
- The Trinity
- Family life & relationships
- Contextualising the gospel into the Muslim mind-set

Mentoring through cultural issues...
- Truth & honesty (Mat.5:37)
- Righteousness in finances (Amos 5:12)
- Legalism versus grace (Galatians)
- Marriage & family relationships
- Charms (Deut.17:10-11)
- Blessings, curses and vows - discernment about potential demonic activity in their situation
- Freedom from the unhelpful aspects of the past (Acts 19:18-20)

Fellowship:

- If it is inappropriate for a new believer to attend public church gatherings, then a home-based group would be safer and less provocative to other concerned Muslims. The key issue here is that, wherever we are, we are 'church', whether it is church gathered in worship or church scattered in the community (see 1 Cor.12:27; 3:16-17; Heb.10:25).

- Local churches being used by God to nurture believers from Islam usually display the following characteristics ...

a) open & caring communities

b) relating to the whole person outside the formal meeting setting

c) culturally flexible like the early church in Acts 6

d) ability to be a surrogate family or alternative 'Umma' (community), which is explored more in *Joining the Family* (see Appendix 3)

Water baptism:

When my family used to pray secretly for my father to come to Christ, he would develop bad moods and become aggressive as a reaction to the Holy Spirit speaking to him.

I have also known baptism in water to be the point at which persecution starts whether others in the community know about it or not. This is a disturbance in the spiritual realm where the enemy can provoke people around the new believer because they themselves are open to such dark influence. But even when a Muslim family does know about a baptism, it is seen as the initiation into 'joining Christianity'.

Worship:

- One question we will face with new believers is whether or not we use alcoholic wine for Communion.

- To have Muslim background believers in western churches may mean a need to encourage young women to dress more modestly, particularly in the summer months.

- For those from a traditional Muslims background it may offend them to see us put a Bible on the floor or prop a church piano up with it. These Muslims will be more comfortable seeing any holy book covered up and not have verses underlined. However, younger westernised Muslims may be more likely to be impressed that a Bible is well used and written in.

- How might believers from Islam affect and/or be affected by our worship-style? For example public hugging and shows of affection, dancing. These are issues to be thought through.

Authority:

- Some males may gravitate to male authority figures in the church and struggle with the idea of relating to 'ordinary' members of the flock.

- We need to wean the new believer away from the Christian mentor and into the wider fellowship of believers.

- Sometimes spiritual deliverance may be needed from 'controlling' spiritual influences or from dabbling in magical practices.

Cross-cultural relationships:

- Some Muslim males from a more traditional background may need time to learn to relate naturally with females in a fellowship. They have a journey to make to unlearn their years of relating to women within Islam in an assumed dominant or superior way.

- In the present western political climate the right to stay in the West is a prized thing and can sometimes be achieved by a marriage certificate. When nurturing believers from Islam we need commonsense and a shrewd, realistic approach to the possibility of a hidden agenda.

- While not resisting such liaisons out of some kind of unbending principle, we need to be ready to advise on cross-cultural relationships, which may form.

- Both parties should go into this with eyes wide open and seriously think through the implications. There needs to be an openness to test God's will in the matter.

- It is advisable to bring in either an established believer from Muslim background and/or an experienced Christian with cross-cultural experience in an Islamic culture.

Believers in Jesus from a Muslim family background face a journey that is fairly unique and certainly very different to the experience of most western followers of Jesus. In fact for Muslim background believers their change of heart-allegiance to Jesus can have an impact that's almost as great as gender-reassignment surgery. Potentially the individual's whole 'identity' (i.e. internal and external) is likely to change. Their network of relationships may be decimated leaving them marginalised and alone. Then there is the process of adjustment of their worldview and how they negotiate their life-decisions.

Friendship First is the first in a trio of books called '*The Friendship Trio*'. *The Friendship First* Course[1] is an interactive small-group introduction to the issues. It will take you through the basics and equip you to put this book into practice.

The other two resources in the trio are *Joining the Family* Course[2] which identifies the needs of new believers from Muslim family backgrounds and how groups of Christians can receive and support them within the context of a local church network.

The third member of the trio is *Come Follow Me*[3] which is a work-book to use as a tool in a one-on-one mentoring situation. It is thoroughly Bible-based and has been carefully prepared and piloted with new believers in various parts of the Muslim world. It facilitates an 'ordinary' Christian to act as a 'spiritual-mentor' to an 'ordinary' believer from a Muslim family background. '*The Friendship Trio*' is available from Kitab Interserve Resources http://kitab.org.uk/trio

The journey of new believers of Muslim background is an arduous one because they have lost the approval and support of part or all of their family – and even their community. They need to be received into a new 'spiritual community' (i.e. Ummah) and the local church is well placed to become that, as long as a group can equip themselves to do it, which is where *Joining the Family* comes into its own.

Christians in local churches can become like an adoptive family for these ·new believers. It's a time-consuming commitment that has to be intentional or it doesn't happen. However an increasing number of Christians are making themselves available for this ministry. So while it's "friendship first" – it's "family" second.

Sources:

1 S. Bell & T. Green, *Friendship First*, Kitab Interserve Resources, 2011

2 T. Green & Roxy, *Joining the Family*, Kitab Interserve Resources, 2016

3 T. Green, *Come Follow Me*, www.lulu.com, 2013

APPENDICES

APPENDIX 1

The Nicene Creed

We believe in one God
The Father the Almighty;
Maker of heaven and earth –
of all that is seen and unseen.

We believe in one Lord Jesus Christ
The only Son of God;
Eternally begotten of the Father,
God from God, light from light
True God from true God,
Begotten not made;
Of one being with the Father
By whom all things were made.

For us men and for our salvation
He came down from heaven.
By the power of the Holy Spirit
He became incarnate of the Virgin Mary
and was made man.

For our sakes he was crucified under
Pontius Pilate. He suffered death and was
buried.

On the third day he rose from the dead
in accordance with the scriptures. He
ascended into heaven and is seated at the
right hand of the Father.

He will come again in glory to judge
Both the living and the dead, and his
kingdom will have no end.

A Muslim Response

We are required to believe in one God
Supreme and unknowable but for 99
Beautiful Names.
He is maker of heaven and earth and all
Worlds and beings - men, angels and *jinn*
spirits.

We must believe in one Holy Qu'ran
The miraculous and final message from
God:
A perfect conception eternally present
with God.
It descended supernaturally for our
guidance.
It was begotten not made.
It proceeded from God by Whom all
things were made.

The Holy Qu'ran was delivered by
dictation of the Angel Gabriel to the
illiterate Prophet Muhammad (peace be
upon him), who recited it to scribes, who
wrote it down. The Holy Qu'ran is the
final revelation of all the previous holy
books i.e. *tawrat* (Torah) of Moses, *zabur*
(Psalms) of David and *injil* (Gospel) of
Jesus. These books emanate from the
'Eternal Tablet' in heaven.

The Prophet Jesus (peace be upon him)
was conceived supernaturally and born of
the Virgin Maryam. He was sinless, unlike
the other prophets.

He did not die but another substituted for
him while he was taken safely to heaven.
The Prophet Jesus (peace be upon him)
will come again to marry, have a family,
be a judge and a martyr for Islam.

We believe in the Holy Spirit
The Lord and Giver of Life
Who proceeds from the Father and the Son.
With the Father and the Son
He is worshipped and glorified.
He has spoken through the Prophets.

We must believe in total submission to God based on fear (the highest religious sentiment), which is demonstrated by the performance of Six Pillars of duty. These are the source and way of Muslim life...

1. Shahada (Creed) *There is no god but God and Muhammad is the apostle of God'*.
2. Salah (x5 per day)
3. Fasting
4. Zakat (2.5% tithe)
5. Hajj (pilgrimage)
6. Jihad (struggle in the way of God)

We believe in one holy catholic and apostolic Church.
We acknowledge one baptism for the forgiveness of sins.
We look for the resurrection of the dead and the Life of the world to come. AMEN

We must believe in one "Ummah" or household of Islam. It is both catholic in its duty of belief and practise which is one;
It is apostolic in its mission to the world until the Judgement Day when all men (Muhammad included) will be at the mercy of God and must await their fate.

APPENDIX 2

Useful Words & Explanations

A

Abrogation

This is a law of Qur'anic interpretation, which stresses the chronology of a verse *(aya)*. Wherever there is apparent contradiction between verses, the later revelation *(nasikh)* is given prime of place over the earlier revelation *(mansukh)* (S2.106; 16.101; 22.52). A valid question to politely ask a Muslim friend is whether God changed his mind. The reason why there is the need to abrogate verses in the first place is neither asked nor answered in Muslim teaching.

Allah

The relationship between God in the Bible and Qur'an is a complex one, which needs a fuller explanation. This is available in Appendix 6.

El	the ancient high god of the Middle East
Elah (Dan.2:45)	Aramaic word for God (Yahweh)
El-yohn (Gen.14:18-20)	Hebrew word for 'Most High God' (Yahweh)
'alah (the root of El-Elyon)	Hebrew word "to ascend" or "be high"
El-ilah or **Allah**	Arabic word for 'High God'

For example 'Allah' can be taken to be the God of Israel on the basis of semantics (i.e. the meaning of words). *Allah* is the Arabic word for God. It was used long before Islam arrived, which is why some of Muhammad's relatives were called things like "Abdullah" (servant/slave of God). Allah is used by millions of Arabic speaking Christians today.

The word comes from *el-illah* (the God); *El* being the word used for the High God throughout several Middle Eastern lands for centuries before Abraham. This is why we find the Hebrew names of Yahweh in the Bible to include *El-Elyon, El-shaddai* etc. The name *Allah* did not need introducing in the Qur'an; it was already known.

In the pagan Arabian Peninsular at the time of Muhammad, the planets were deified. Not surprisingly Allah, although being the High God, was also identified with the moon. Allah was also understood to be the overseer of a dynasty of lesser gods amongst which Allah had three daughters, Al-Lat, Al-Uzza and Menat (S37.149-153; 16.59; 17:41-42). These deities were worshipped along with Satan and the *jinn* (S4.116,117; 6.100).

Those who say that Allah is not the God and Father of our Lord Jesus Christ are right if they mean that god is not so described by Muslims. They are wrong if they mean that Allah is other than the God of the Christian faith.

Kenneth Cragg

If Allah is the God of Israel semantically, the next issue is whether the spiritual reality behind the name "Allah" is the same as that behind the name "El". The apologist says it is but quickly qualifies that by recognising that as the sword entered Islam in Medina so some form of darkness occurred as an increasingly politicised Islam grew. It is clear that a particularly violent spiritual principality is present today in the Islamic system. Surely the actions of violent Muslims could no more turn Allah into a demon god than the actions of violent Christians during the Crusades could turn the God of the Bible into a demon god. This is an unfortunate misconception and seems to be the root of the confusion.

> The difference between a Muslim and a Christian's perception of God is the difference between an Englishman and a Corsican's perception of the Sun. - i.e. the Englishman sees only clouds and dimmed light and warmth. The Corsican enjoys the full warmth, heat and light. This is a radically different perception of the same thing due to their differing vantage points.

Some scholars argue that what Muhammad began in sincerity and spiritual purity, his wife Khadijah and his close companions developed in a politicised way after Muhammad's death. We know that Muhammad was persecuted for trying to wean the idol-worshipping Arab tribes away from their gods to the worship of the one God - Allah (S38.4).

Muhammad himself further strengthened this case when he insisted that Allah is the God of Abraham and the Jews when he asserted 'Our God and your God is One; and it is to Him we bow' (S3.84; 29.46). This helps explain why some Muslims resent the Christian insinuation that the early idolatrous connections with the moon are also seen in the crescent moon, which has become the adopted symbol of Islam. In reality this symbol has more to do with the fact that the Islamic year, like Judaism, follows a lunar calendar. It is true that a traditional drink to break the fast in Ramadan is called *Qamar al-Din* (Moon of religion). However, this point can be interpreted either way.

People who love, interpret the facts about the one they love more accurately than those who do not love. When our eyes see badly we only notice the darker aspects of what we observe.

John Chrysostom

The question as to whether Allah is the God of the Bible is a trick question in that it is like asking "Have you stopped beating your wife yet?" I am trapped whatever I say. The question is therefore best answered by asking some other questions…

1 Is the Muslim idea about God the same as the Bible? - No
2 Is there anything in common between the Muslim & Bible ideas of God? - Yes
3 Is there enough in common for us to be able to use the same word? - Yes

On the bases of the above answers we can ask the counter question "Is the Jesus of the Jehovah's Witnesses the Christ of the Gospels?". The answer has to be "yes" because there is only one Jesus but their understanding of him is faulty.

- Paul in Athens referred to a pagan 'Unknown god' as *theos* (Acts 17:3), not necessarily because of the identity of that god but because what is in the Greek mind is close enough to the God he is referring to.

- Paul's assumption is that there can only be one High God under discussion. Experience of Muslim enquirers, and believers in Jesus from Islam, gives us confidence that we are in fact talking about the same thing.

- Believers from Islam have stated that, in Christ, they have come to know Allah for the first time. They have found completion in Christ.
- Traditional Sunni Islam teaches that Allah is unknowable. This called

into question by the experience of a high-born Pakistani believer from Muslim background, Bilquis Sheikh. In her book *'I Dared to call Him Father'* she experiences Allah personally. This indicates that – for her – He is both personally knowable and also the same person as the God of the Bible. Through Christ, she found the God of the Qur'an who she had been trying to worship from a respectable Islamic distance all her life.

- Traditional Sunni Islam teaches that Allah is unknowable. However, the book *I Dared to call Him Father* is the story of Pakistani lady Bilquis Sheikh. This is an example of continuity rather than discontinuity. Through Christ, she found the God she had worshipped from a respectable Islamic distance all her life.

- It is therefore more helpful to see Allah as the God of the Bible but that the Muslim understanding of Him is faulty.

- Yes there is darkness within the Islamic system but to conclude that Allah is a demonic principality to be shunned by the Muslim is confusing for them and only makes the gulf between them and the truth bigger.

- Patient explanation from the Bible is the only way to help believers from Islam to move from the Arab to the Judeo-Christian understanding of God avoiding a mixture of both understandings (syncretism).
  n.b. Jesus is not only *Emmanu-Yahweh* (i.e. of the Jews) but *Emmanu-El* (the high god with us). The uniqueness of Jesus is His claim to be El and therefore the High God of the universe and the Lord of Life.

C   Creation - What do Muslims believe?

Unlike the six days of creation in the Torah and Bible, different Suras of the Qur'an teach the creation of the world in a different numbers of days. In contrast to the Bible, the impression is given more clearly in the Qur'an that a 'day' does not necessarily mean 24 hours. Today, Muslims tend to support any science, which supports the Qur'anic view of the order, balance and purpose of the created world.

Communism & Islam

Islam has similarities with Communism. Both have the idea of the corporate society *(Ummah)*. Both are committed to the equality of all individuals

in an egalitarian way. Both regulate society very firmly according to a set creed established by a charismatic founder. Both punish severely departure from the
set doctrine. Political liaisons between the two are not unknown, for example Syria. It is not unreasonable to think of Islam as 'spiritual communism'.

D

Dynamic Equivalents

These are devices to help our Muslim friend grasp Bible truth. For example the issue under discussion between the Qur'an and the Bible is not Muhammad versus Jesus. The dynamic equivalent of Muhammad in Christianity is Mary not Jesus.

- The Qur'an is the 'word made book' while Jesus is the 'word made flesh'.

- Muhammad gave birth to the word made book' and Mary gave birth to the 'word made flesh.

F

Feast Days - on which to make contact

The Arabic word for "feast" is *Eid*, which means "returning at regular intervals". These are usually public holidays in Muslim countries. It goes down well to greet Muslims on feast days with the words in Arabic *"Eid al-mubarak!"* (Blessed feast to you!). You can find out the dates of the feasts from your Muslim contact. Here are the more important feasts.

- **Eid ul-Adha** (Feast of Sacrifice)
  Commemorates Abraham's near sacrifice of his son. Islamic tradition says it was 'Ishmael' while the Bible clearly says it was Isaac (Gen.22). On this occasion a sheep or goat (1 per household), cow or camel (1 per 7 households) is sacrificed in an *halal* fashion. One third of the meat is consumed by the household covered and the remainder is distributed to friends or the poor.
- **Lailat ul-Bara'at** (Night of full-moon before Ramadan - 14 Shabaan)
- **Ramadan** (a lunar month)
  Designated to the annual fast from sunrise to sunset
- **Lailat ul-Qadr** (Night of Power - 27 Ramadan)
  The night near the end of the month of Ramadan when Muslims believe Gabriel began to reveal the Qur'an to Muhammad. Muslims are sometimes open to specially answered prayer

and the supernatural assistance of God at this time. Millions
of Christians are now praying for Muslims during Ramadan
and supernatural intervention is being reported in the lives of
ordinary Muslims.

- **Eid ul-Fitr** (Feast of Breaking the Fast)
  Literally in Arabic, 'Feast of Breakfast'. A three or four day feast
  commemorates the end of the fasting month of Ramadan. This
  is the closest atmosphere the Muslim world gets to the western
  Christmas. Children often have new clothes and presents can be
  exchanged.
- **Lailat ul-Miraj** (Miraculous Night Journey 27 Rajab)
  A one-night event where devout Muslims meditate and reflect
  on Muhammad's supernatural journey.
- **Mawlid an-Nabbi** (Muhammad's birthday - 12 Rabi al-awwal)
  Devout Muslims commemorate Muhammad's life and
  achievements.
- **Muharram** (Muslim New Year, first month in the Islamic
  calendar)
  A bank holiday in Muslim countries.
- **10 Muharram** or Ashura (Shi'ite memorial of the martyrdom of
  Hussein)
- **Hajj** (Lunar month designated to pilgrimage to Mecca)
  Most Hajj pilgrims will set out for Mecca in this month as it is
  thought to carry maximum *baraka* (blessing)

G **The Gospel of Barnabas**

Muslims struggle with the idea of four written Gospels and their tradition
says the original *Injil* (Gospel) was lost. It is assumed that Christians
concocted four Gospels to replace the original. Some Muslims argue for
the authenticity of a document first found in the Papal Library around
1590. It is now called the Gospel of Barnabas. It seems to have been
written by an Italian between 1400-1500AD - probably a convert to
Islam. The document attempts to endorse the Qur'an's version of the life
and work of Jesus. The writer is someone who had knowledge of the
'apocryphal' traditions of both Christianity and Islam but little clue about
the geography nor the historical context of Jesus or Muhammad. Its details
therefore contradict both New Testament and Qur'an. The writer claims
to be Barnabas and that he associated with Jesus. The real Barnabas was
only associated with Paul. This so-called 'Muslim Gospel' is a jumble of
inaccuracies and even quotes from the work of the writer Dante who did
not live until 1245-1321 AD.

H   Hygiene

Nasal discharge is thought by many Muslim cultures to be as unclean as urine or faeces. When a Muslim has a cold it is not uncommon for them to sniff rather than wipe or blow the nose. This is seen as more appropriate in a toilet. It is more common to spit or blow the nose outside as this does not make a house unclean.

M   Meccan & Medinan Suras

The Meccan suras were written in Mecca during the phase of Muhammad's career when the Muslim community were an opposed minority. These suras tend to be more reasoned and deal with spiritual issues that resonate with the concerns expressed by the minor prophets of the Old Testament. I have read such suras to Bible College students and asked which minor prophet it is and they have taken the question seriously and searched their Bibles before I told them it was actually from the Qur'an.

All other suras were 'received' in Medina. They tend to be more volatile and even aggressive in tone during a phase when the Muslim community was in the majority and powerful.

Mosque

Masjid is the word in Arabic. It is the 'gathering' or 'meeting' place and centre of the worshipping Muslim community.

Inside a mosque:

- There is a place to perform *wudu* (ritual washing).

- The men and women worship in separate areas screened off from one another. The women usually pray behind the men and sometimes even have their own entrance.

- The focal-point is the *mihrab*. This is a highly decorated recess in a wall giving the precise direction of Mecca. The wall in which this recess is built is called the *qiblah*.

- Sermons are preached from a *mimbar* (pulpit).

The usage of the mosque:
- Officially there is no clergy or hierarchy within Islam. Prayers can be led by anyone who becomes the *imam* - this can be simply a reliable and experienced Muslim, though it tends to be the well read Muslims who become known as *sheikh* (elder) or *mu'allam* (teacher). These are like rabbi figures.

- Mosques often run after-school Qur'anic classes to teach Muslim youngsters their faith. This is called a *madrasa* (school). Some Muslim boys can recite the Qur'an by heart by their fourteenth birthday.

- Some mosques also provide recreational facilities for Muslim young people.

N Names

Naming is a complex business in Muslim cultures. Names can come from the area of family origin, or from their family clan or their grand father or father's name. For example Usama bin Muhammad bin Laden means Usama "son of" Muhammad (his father) "son of" Laden (his grand father i.e. family name).

Males can change their name if they are seriously ill in the belief that this will confuse the *jinn* spirits who may wish to take advantage and kill them.

Boys names are often taken from …
1 the prophets of the Qur'an e.g. Ibrahim, Musa or Muhammad
2 the 'companions' of Muhammad e.g. Ali, Usman or Abu Bakr
the names of God e.g. Rahman, Rashid

Girls are often named after …
1 the honourable women mentioned in the Qur'an e.g. Sara or Maryam
2 the women from Muhammad's family e.g. Fatima or Khadijah
3 the names of God e.g. Azizah or Mahbubah
4 beautiful things in their native languages e.g. Shukria or Shireen

Women may change their names several times through their life. For instance when they complete adolescence, when they marry and by the name of the first born son (Oum Ahmad or Mother of Ahmad).

P Proclamatory Dialogue

This is not a theologically liberal stance, which might tempt us to go in search of points of agreement and compromise at all cost. Like the liberal stance, this form of dialogue does involve listening and genuinely trying to understand and learn. However, it differs in that it also involves having something to say (proclaim) in response to what we hear and learn from our Muslim friend.

The evangelical position is sometimes seen as bigoted and closed to the

'truth' of others. The fact is that, like the old saying, Christians are only 'beggars sharing bread'. This is the balance of proclamatory dialogue i.e.
...

a We are *beggars* relating in humility.

b We are *sharing* in dia-logue not dictating in mono-logue.

c There is such a thing as the objective *bread* of life to share.

R Redemptive Analogy

Simply put, these are analogies of redemption. That is to say they are devices, which use what my Muslim friend knows and building on it to convey the truth about Jesus. Here are two examples...

- The Black Stone
  This is a smooth corner of old meteorite rock on which the Ka'aba is built in Mecca. It is the centre of hajj pilgrimage and Muslim veneration. The stone is black and shiny, which has led to the tradition that it became shiny and smooth by the kisses and stroking of millions of pilgrims and that it is black because when pilgrims kiss it their sins are transferred to it. Psalm 2 says 'kiss the Son'. Jesus is the Black Stone of Christianity. When we embrace Him by faith our sin is dealt with.

- Abraham's sacrifice
  In Genesis 22 Abraham is willing to offer his only son. Muslim tradition says it is Ishmael but it really doesn't matter. The issue is the ram in the thicket. The story outlines 'substitutionary atonement'. Jesus is the Lamb of God and was slain to save us from being slain and bring us into relationship with God.

S Sharia

This is the name given to Islamic Law, which is a parallel to the Old Testament law. The Arabic word *sharia* means pathway. It was used for the pathways leading to water holes in the desert. Such a beautiful concept seems far from the reality that wherever sharia law has been attempted in modern times, it has introduced economic ruin, or political chaos or bloodshed, or all three; for example Iran, Sudan, Pakistan and Nigeria.

Sharia Law legislates for all human behaviour. Sin, personal vice and crime are all treated as one issue under the divine rule. The four sources of authority in Sharia Law are ...

1 *qur'an* - the revealed scripture
2 *hadith* - the Traditions about Muhammad's life
3 *ijma* - judgement based on the consensus of qualified persons
4 *qias* - judgement based on the use of analogies with other cases

The theory behind sharia law is that, as the revelation of God, it provides everything the Muslim can ever need to determine how he or she should live. Sharia is a guide and bench-mark for everyday life. Some people compare Islam to "spiritual communism" when this sort of prescriptive framework is extended to the regulation of Muslim society. There are four different schools of interpretation of Sharia Law. The four sharia schools are …
a Hanifi
b Hanbali
c Shafi
d Maliki

The schools can cause controversy within a Muslim community. For example the huge internal disagreement as to how to respond to Salman Rushdie's book 'The Satanic Verses'. The differing schools can also create legal wrangling. For instance if a Muslim is not satisfied with one ruling he can go to a lawyer of another school to get the ruling he likes.

Source of Islam
The $64,000 question is - "What is the origin of Islam?". This is not easy to answer, however it possible to narrow the field a bit and say that it can only come from one of three sources.
1 divine revelation
2 human conception
3 satanic imitation

Life is never straightforward and it is highly likely that Islam is actually a mixture. This calls for mature discernment on the part of Christians trying to befriend a Muslim.

Apart from the 'spiritual sources' of Islam, the reasons for its birth and rapid development are various. However, we must remember that all of them, whether good, bad or indifferent, they fall within the sovereign purpose of God and therefore must somehow have a place in the divine economy as do wars, natural disasters, the Crusades, the holocaust, Hiroshima or Apartheid. The following pointers may be helpful.
1 The failure of a weak church of the time that was lacking in understanding of the Scriptures, moral purity and mission vision.
2 Islam as an 'Arabised' form of Judaism appealed to the Semitic Arabs.
3 Islam spread quickly largely along natural Arab trading routes and through

what Christians today call 'tentmaking'.

4 Islam spread by political, economic and military force

5 Islam has spread through significant population growth

W The place of women in Islam

It is clear that Islam, like the Old Testament, reveals a male-oriented culture. For example it is interesting to note that the Virgin Mary *(Maryam)* is the only woman to be mentioned in the Qur'an by name. In Islamic law, women tend to be held in a tension between being dutifully 'protected' and negatively oppressed. The women of Muslim societies have been called the "wind-sock" of the Muslim World. How they are treated is a clear indicator of which way the wind the wind is blowing in any given situation. For example the harsh regime in Afghanistan under the Taliban was hard on women. This cultural practise comes partly from the same culture as the Old Testament where the honour and wealth of a family could be assessed by the number, modesty and chastity of its women.

However, it is right to point out that there appears to have been more involvement of women in the life of the Old Testament community than is true in conservative Muslim societies (see Deut.29:9-13; Neh.8:1-3; 2 Kgs.4;23; 22:12-20; Judges 4:4-5:31). Jesus' treatment of women was clearly preferential and emerged out of his relationship with them (see Mt.22:30; 27:55-56; Mk.12:40-44; Lk.7:36-50; Jn.4:7-27, 12:3-8).

Modesty:
In conservative Islam, women should not look at men nor reveal any of their body to a male other than her close family (S24.31). Women are to remain in the home and whenever they go out to cover modestly with the *hijab* (S33.33). The hijab was originally a head covering but has traditionally grown to become total covering *(purdah)* in some Muslim societies.

Spiritually:
According to the Hadith most of those who go to hell will be women. (Bukhari Vol.1, pgs 48 & 301). Women are deficient in intelligence, religion and gratitude (Bukhari Vol.1, No.301)

Legal rights:
The Qur'an says ... *'women shall have rights similar to the rights against them...but men have a degree over them'* (S2.228). Another aspect of this legal inequality is the fact that a woman's inheritance rights are half that of a man... *'To the male a portion equal to that of two females'* (S4.11) *'... and if there are not two men, then a man and two women such as you*

choose for witness' (S2.282) and again... *'In what you leave (i.e. in legacy) the wife's share is a fourth if you leave no children; but if you leave a child the wife gets an eighth, after payment of legacies and debts'* (S4.12).

In Christianity the Apostle Peter writes that *'women are the weaker vessel'* (1 Pet.3:7). Sadly the reflection in Islamic tradition, is that the woman's dependency on the senior males in the household is ...because of the *'deficiency of a woman's mind* (Hadith Vol 3:826). A husband may therefore punish an errant wife... *'Women on whose part you fear disloyalty and ill-conduct, admonish them and refuse to share their beds, beat them.'* (S4.34).

Sexual practises:

One Hadith reports Muhammad as saying *'When a man marries, he perfects half of religion'*. The Qur'an says *'Marry women of your choice, two or three or four.'* (S4.3). There are also some disturbing references to women and sexual behaviour. For example *'The Prophet (i.e. Muhammad) married A'isha when she was six years old and co-habited with her when she was nine'*. Another Hadith (Vol 6:51) says *'The Jews used to say if one has sexual intercourse with his wife from the back she will deliver a squint-eyed child; so this verse was revealed. 'Your wives are a tilth (i.e. ploughed field). So approach her when and how you will'* (see S2.223).

Women are seen as the possession of their husbands for his enjoyment (S3.14). A Muslim man may marry up to four wives provided he can treat them all equally (S4.3), which the Qur'an admits is impossible (S4.129).

APPENDIX 3

Resources

General assistance:

Global Connections
Caswell Road, Sydenham Industrial Estate, Leamington Spa, CV31 1QF
Tel: 01926 487755
email: info@globalconnections.co.uk
For general help including access to the full list of organisations with expertise
and experience in this field.

Prayer for Muslims:

30 Days of Prayer for the Muslim World
www.30daysprayer.org.uk

FFM – (Fellowship of Faith for Muslims)
PO Box 8943, Nottingham, NG4 9BB
For a monthly bulletin of information for prayer and an annual prayer
conference.

Study Courses for Christians:

The Friendship Trio
available from kitab.org.uk/trio
> Friendship First – a small group video course helping Christians discuss
> good news with Muslim people
> www.friendshipfirst.org
> Joining the Family – a small group video course for ordinary churches
> helping them receive people from Muslim backgrounds into fellowship
> www.joiningthefamily.org
> Come follow Me – a 1-on-1 discipling manual for people from Muslim
> backgrounds who are following Jesus

All Nations Christian College Islamics Course
Easneye, Ware, Herts SG12 8IX
Tel: 01920 461243,
email: info@allnations.ac.uk

The Prophet Stories
By Jan Pike. A resource which enables groups of Muslim and Christian

people to talk about what we understand about God, through the listening of and telling of the same prophet's story from both the Qur'an and the Bible. Available after attendance at a one day seminar.
email: info@prophetstories.org.uk

Audio Resources:

Language Recordings
PO Box 197, High Wycombe HP14 3YY
Tel: 01494 485 414
email: irukoffice@aol.com

Biographies of converted Muslims:

I Dared to Call Him Father
Bilquis Sheikh, Waco, TX., Word Books, 1978
An excellently written account of a high born Pakistani lady finding Christ

Into the Light
Stephen Masood, OM, 1986
A sincere Muslim scholar follows Christ

Jesus: more than a Prophet
RWF Wooton (ed.), Inter-Varsity Press, Leicester, 1982. Fifteen Muslims find forgiveness, release and new life

The Fifth Pillar of Islam
David Zeidan, AWM

The Torn Veil & Beyond the Veil
Gulshan Esther, Marshall Pickering
Two books telling the story of a Pakistani woman who followed Jesus and then was miraculously healed.

Seeking Allah Finding Jesus
Nabeel Qureishi, Zondervan, 2014
An American Ahmadi man finds Jesus through a year-long debate with a Christian friend

The Imam's Daughter
Hannah Shah, Rider, 2009
The story of a young British Pakistani girl's escape to freedom

Hiding in the Light
Rifqa Bary, Waterbrook Press, 2015
An American Sri Lankan girl risks everything to follow Jesus

Against the Grain
Khalad Hussain, Xlibris Publishing, 2012

Outlets for literature for use with Muslims:

CPO (Christian Publicity Organisation)
Garcia Estate, Canterbury Road, Worthing, BN13 1BW
Tel: 01903 263 354
email: info@cpo.org.uk
For greetings cards featuring appropriate Bible texts in Muslim languages

Elam Ministries
For a wide range of resources and training for Iranians and Afghans,
shop.kalameh.com

Kitab - Interserve Resources
5-6 Walker Avenue, Wolverton Mill, Milton Keynes, MK12 5TW,
email: sales@kitab.org.uk
The biggest national supplier of materials about Islam, from a basic level to
academic. Also for written and audio-visual materials for use with people who
speak vernacular Muslim languages. www.kitab.org.uk

SGM Lifewords (former Scripture Gift Mission International)
1A The Chandlery, 50 Westminster Bridge Road, London SE1 7QY
Tel: 020-7730-2155
email: uk@sgmlifewords.com

Word of Life
P O Box 14, Oldham, OL1 3WW
Diglot Scripture Calendars & Bible Correspondence Course to help a Muslim
learn about the Christian Faith; also used to nurture a Christian from a Muslim
background.

Christian Organisations:

Agape (Jesus Video)
167 Newhall Street, Birmingham, B3 1SW
Tel: 0121 765 4404,
email: info@agape.org.uk

The Jesus Video is obtainable in most Muslim languages.

Alliance of Asian Christians
Carr's Lane Church Centre, Carrs Lane, Birmingham B4 7SX
Tel: 0121 633 4533

Asian Equip
297 Haslucks Green Rd, Shirley, Solihull, B90 1PE
Tel: 0121 744 3057

South Asian Concern
5 Vernon Rise, Kings Cross, london, WC1X 9EP
Tel: 020 7683 0618
southasianconcern.org
Encouraging, equipping and enabling followers of Jesus into more effective
engagement with South Asians; helping South Asian first generation believers
respect their family's heritage and culture in the way they follow Jesus.

When Women Speak
www.whenwomenspeak.net
email: admin@whenwomenspeak.net

Islamic Organisations:

The Muslim Educational Trust
130, Stroud Green Road, London N4 3RZ
email: info@muslim-ed-trust.org.uk
For authentic information from a Muslim source

Islamic Presentation Centre International (IPCI)
434 Coventry Road, Birmingham B10 OUG
Tel: 0121 773 0137 Fax: 0121 766 8577
email: info@ipci-iv.co.uk
n.b. Also an online shop www.islamicvision.co.uk/index.php
For a mail order catalogue of literature on most issues from a Muslim
perspective, also to order a Qur'an.

Islamic Publications:

Islamic Quarterly Magazine
Islamic Cultural Centre & Central Mosque, 146, Park Road,
London NW8 7RG
www.iccuk.org
For an authentic journal from a Muslim source.

Christian Websites to help Muslims enquiring about Jesus:

www.answering-islam.org (n.b. there are links to many more sites from this site)
www.bibleandkoran.org
www.injil.org

Stories of the Prophets
Al-Massira is a course used with Middle Eastern Muslim people who are interested in Jesus. It gives a chronological overview of the prophets in the Bible finding fulfilment in Jesus. After attending Al Massira training you can lead a course. almassira.org

Christian Websites to help followers of Jesus from a Muslim Background:

Christianity explained to Muslims
www.arabicbible.com/for-muslims/christianity-explained.html

Christianity & Islam in dialogue
www.bibleandkoran.org

Joining the Family
www.joiningthefamily.org

Muslim Websites:

General sites
www.islamic.org.uk
www.al-islam.org

Propogation Centre
www.ipci-iv.co.uk

Council on Islamic-American Relations
www.cair.com

Islamic Gateway
www.ummah.com

Muslim Directory
www.muslimdirectory.co.uk

World Assembly of Muslim Youth
www.wamy.co.uk

APPENDIX 4

Islamic Words & Expressions

A

abd	A male slave
abrogation	A principle of Qu'ranic interpretation (see Useful Explanations)
ahl-al-kitab	People of the Book i.e. Jews and Christians
Allah	The Arabic word for God
al-hamdu lilah	Arabic for "Praise be to God" i.e. 'Praise the Lord!'
al-asr	The afternoon prayer time
arkan-ud-din	The pillars of religion i.e. the Five Pillars of Islam
athaan	The call to prayer
ayah	Used for a verse of the Qur'an. The Arabic for 'sign'. Ayat in Urdu.
Ayatollah	A term of honour for a *Shiah* religious leader. Literally 'sign of Allah'

B

baraka	Blessing
begum	Pakistani word in the Urdu language. A respected married woman.
bismillah	Arabic for "In the name of God". Used before a Muslim does anything
burqa	Pakistani Urdu term for ladies clothing that covers the whole body including hands and face.

C

Caliph	Derived form the Arabic name *khalifa* or ruler of a Muslim community.
chador	The Persian word for *burqa*, the ladies clothing covering the whole body

D   *dahwah*   Literally "invitation" or "appeal" and used for Islamic mission

dar ul-harb   The house of war i.e. the non-Muslim world

dar ul-islam   The house of Islam

din   Arabic for religion (i.e. the outward practice)

du'a   Petitionary prayer

dhimmi   All non-Muslims living in a Muslim country. Subjugated and sometimes forced to pay a tax (see *jizya*)

E   *Eid*   Feast

Eid-ul-fitr   The feast of "break-fast", which marks the end of Ramadan, the lunar fasting month

Eid-ul-adha   The name for the Sheep Feast. Also called *Eid-ul-kibir*. This is observed 70 days after the end of Ramadan

Eid-ul-milad   The name for the feast of the official birth of Muhamad and also of the birth of Jesus (Christmas)

F   *fajr*   The early morning prayer time

falah   Self effort and positive achievement

fatiha   The opening chapter (*sura*) of the Qur'an

fatwa   A published decision on a matter of Islamic law

H   *hadith al-qudsi*   An individual "holy tradition" or trustworthy report on an action or opinion of Muhammad (see *hadith*)

hadith	The second holy book of Islam containing the *hadith al-qudsi*, a collection of traditions about the life and work of Muhamad. (see *isnad*)
hafiz	Someone who has memorised the Koran. Also a professional Koranic reciter
hajj	The annual pilgrimage to Mecca and Medina (see *hajji*)
hajji	Someone who has been on hajj. Men may dye their beards henna orange as a sign of this distinction (see *hajj*)
halal	Muslim equivalent of Jewish kosher food. Also used of food i.e. animal meat or fats obtained by slaughter invoking the name of God. Also something that is lawful and permissible.
haram	Something that is forbidden e.g. pork and alcohol. Also used for "shame on you" when someone does something inappropriate
harem	The female section of a Muslim household
higra	Muhamad's flight from Mecca to Medina happened in 622 AD. This became 1 AH "anno-higra" and marked this start of the Muslim calendar
hijab	An Arabic word for "partition" or "curtain". It is used of the head and face coverings worn my Muslim women
hilel	The crescent moon, symbol of Islam, which like Judaism, is based on the lunar calendar.
hizb	party or group e.g. "*Hizb Allah*", a radical Palestinian group
Iblis	One of the names used for Satan or evil. It is derived from diabolos
iftar	The "breakfast" or evening meal enjoyed by fasting Muslims during Ramadan
ijma	A consensus or opinion of a recognised Islamic authority about the understanding or interpretation of the Qur'an

	imam	The recognised leader of a mosque
	iman	Faith
	Injil	Literally "gospel" or "evangel". The book, which Muslims believe was revealed from God to Jesus
	isha	The last of the five prayer times of the day. Performed after dark
	ISIS	The self-styled terrorist group – 'Islamic State in Iraq and Syria'
	isnad	A chain of people whose credentials lend weight to the reliability of a tradition (see *hadith*).
J	*janna*	Arabic for "garden" and used for Paradise
	jihad	To "struggle in the way of God" (S47.4,77), which can be expressed in doing good or violent acts (see *mujahid*)
	jinn	A spirit entity either good, evil or neutral. They need placating and coercing to help the individual. Unofficial magical practitioners' help.
	jizya	he tax payable by non-Muslims (*dhimmi*) in Muslim lands as a sign of their subservience to the majority culture
	jumma	Friday - the holy day in which prayer is important
K	*ka'aba*	Literally "cube" in Arabic and used of the black draped edifice in the grand mosque in Mecca, a centre of pilgrimage
	kafir	An unbeliever. The opposite of believer - (see *mu'min*)
	kalima	Literally a "statement" used for the Islamic creed "There is no god but God and Muhamad is the apostle of God"

khutba	The sermon by the Imam after the Friday prayers
kismet	The lot in life assigned to the Muslim (fate)
Kitab	Used for both the Koran and the Bible. Literally 'book'
Koran	The holy book of Islam, also spelt "Qur'an". Literally 'Recitation'

L

Lailat al-Qadr	The Feast of the Night of Power observed on the last Friday night of the fasting month of Ramadan

M

Malam	A religious teacher used more in Africa
maghreb	The evening or sunset prayers. Used to name Morocco the most western edge of the Muslim World where the sun sets
Mahdi	A title meaning "the one who is rightly guided". He is almost a Messianic figure who is awaited, particularly by *Shia* Muslims
mansukh	A later revelation in either Qur'an or Hadith, which supersedes an earlier one (see *nasikh*)
matn	The actual text of a *Hadith* (see *isnad*)
Mecca	The birth-place of Muhammad and city of his early life. Now the epi-centre of world Islam and the place of pilgrimage (*see hajj*)
Medina	The city, 200 miles from Mecca, where Muhamad fled persecution to in the *Higra* (emigration). It is also a site for pilgrims.
mihrab	The point on a mosque wall, indicating the direction of Mecca, which is the direction for Muslim prayer (see *qibla*)
minaret	The slender tower attached to a mosque from where the muezzin calls the people to prayer. Today loud speakers are mostly used
miraj	The mystical night-time journey Muhammad is

		believed to have made to heaven. It is rather like the apostle Paul being transported to the seventh heaven
	mizan	The scales on which everyone's good and bad deeds are weighed on Judgement Day (see *Yum al'akhirah*)
	mosque	From the Arabic *masjid* or *gamaa* meaning place of gathering. It is the Muslim equivalent of a church building.
	muezzin	The one who calls Muslims to prayer
	Muharram	The first month in the Islamic calendar.
	mujahid	In one sense all Muslims are *mujahid* as they uphold the five Pillars of Islam. But the term is used specifically to refer to someone who does active *jihad* i.e. a struggle in the way of God - sometimes military. The plural is *mujahideen*
	mu'min	A 'true' believer i.e. practicing, whether Muslim or Christian (see *kafir*)
	Muslim	A male follower of Islam. Literally "one who submits to God".
	Muslima	A female follower of Islam. Literally "one who submits to God".
	Mullah	A religious teacher used more in the Indo-Pakistan sub-continent
N	*nabi*	Arabic for a prophet. Used of Muhammad to persuade Jews of his day that he was in the authentic line of Old Testament prophets
	nasikh	An earlier revelation in Qur'an or Hadith, which is replaced by a later one (see *mansukh*)
P	*pbuh*	Used in brackets after any mention of Muhammad in Muslim literature. It is shorthand for "Peace be upon him"
	pir	A holy person who is saintly

	purdah	Literally "curtain". Used for the seclusion and the veiling of women
Q	*qibla*	The direction Muslims must face to pray i.e. towards Mecca
	Qur'an	The holy book of Islam, also spelt "Koran"
R	*raka'a*	One round of Muslim prayer positions
	Ramadan	The lunar month in the Islamic calendar in which the main fasting takes place
	rasul	An apostle or messenger. One through whom a holy book is revealed. Used of Muhammad to persuade Christians of his day that he was in the authentic line of New Testament apostles
S	*sadaqa*	Voluntary offerings, usually on feast days, given in addition to the regular *zakat* (tithe)
	salah	The ritual prayers of Islam performed five times daily
	salam	The Arabic word for "peace" the counterpart to Hebrew "shalom". It is used as a greeting
	saleeb	The Cross of Christ. Also used for the act of crucifixion
	sawm	Fasting
	shahada	The Islamic creed "There is no god but God and Muhammad is the apostle of God"
	Shariah	Historically used to refer to a desert "path" leading to water. It now refers to Islamic religious law as the 'way' to live
	Shaytan	Satan
	Sheikh	An elder, leader, respectable or learned person in the Muslim community, a good word to attach to an older man's name to show respect. Used by Christian Arabs for a church 'elder'

	Shiah	The Muslim group (*Shi'ites*) that believes the true successor to Muhammad was Ali, his closest male relative
	shirk	The unforgivable sin in Islam of associating a person or an object with God
	Sufi	The word comes from the Arabic "*suf*" (wool). It is used for a Muslim who is committed to experiential and mystical experience of God. The Sufis are also a sect within Islam. In some ways they are the 'charismatics' of Islam
	Sunna	Literally "a trodden pathway". Used of the sayings and doings of Muhammad as found jointly in the Qur'an and the *hadith*
	Sunni	Literally someone who is "of the pathway". An orthodox follower of Islam
	Surah	Literally a "series". Used for a chapter of the Qur'an
T	*Tahrif*	The doctrine that the Bible was corrupted by Jews and Christians
	Talmud	The Jewish traditional law. Could be seen as a parallel to shariah law
	tanzil	Literally "to descend". The process of revelation 'coming down' from heaven
	tasbih	Muslim prayer beads with 33 beads - prayed through three times to give the 99 names of God
	taqdir	Destiny, fate or predestination
	taqiya	Disguising of your true beliefs when you are in a position of weakness
	tawaf	A circumambulation of the *Ka'aba* in Mecca during *hajj* pilgrimage
	Tawrat	The Old Testament in general but the *torah*, i.e. first five books of the Bible, in particular
U	*Ulamma*	The corporate theological community in Islam. The scholars

	Ummah	The worldwide community of Muslims
W	*wahy*	Divine inspiration
	wudu	Ablutions before prayer i.e. washing hands, feet and every orifice of the head
Y	*Yum al-akhirah*	The Last Day i.e. the Day of Judgement
Z	*Zabur*	Psalms
	zakat	Literally "purification". Used for the obligatory charity or tithe to the local mosque
	zuhr	The mid-day prayers i.e. the second of the day

APPENDIX 5

Background & Further Reading

N. Anderson	*Islam in the Modern World – a Christian perspective*, Apollos, 1990
S. Bell	*Grace for Muslims*, Authentic Media, 2006
S. Bell	*Gospel for Muslims*, Authentic Media, 2012
M. Burness	*What do I say to my Muslim Friends*, C.M.S.
E. Challen	*Love your Muslim neighbour*, Day One Publications, 2006
P.G. Chandler	*Pilgrims of Christ on the Muslim Road*, Cowley Publications, 2007
C. Chapman	*You go and do the same – Studies in relating to Muslims*, CMS, BMMF & IFES, 1983
C. Chapman	*Cross & Crescent – Responding the challenge of Islam*, IVP 1995
C. Chapman	*Whose Promised Land?* (revised edition), Lion Books, 2015
C. Darg	*Miracles among Muslims*, Destiny Image, 2006
B. Dennett	*Sharing the Good News with Muslims*, ANZEA Publishers, 1992
D. Garrison	*A Wind in the House of Islam*, WIGTake Resources, 2014
R. George	*Newer Paths in Muslim-Christian Understanding*, Xulon Press, 2007
M. Goldsmith	*Islam & Christian Witness*, Marc Europe, 1987
T. Green & Roxy	*Joining the Family*, Kitab Interserve Resources, 2016
T. Green	*Come Follow Me*, Lulu.com, 2013
I. Glaser	*Thinking Biblically about Islam: Genesis, Transfiguration, Transformation*, Langham Global Library, 2016
J. Goodwin	*What Price Honour*, Plume Books, 2002
P. Jenkins	*God's Continent – Christianity, Islam and Europe's religious Crisis* Oxford University Press, 2009

B. Lewis	*The Crisis of Islam: Holy War & Holy Terror*, Weidenfeld & Nicolson, 2003
R. Love	*Muslims, Magic and the Kingdom of God*, William Carey Library, 2003
C. Medearis	*Muslims, Christians, and Jesus – understanding and building Connections*, Bethany House, 2008
C. Medearis	*Speaking of Jesus – the art of not-evangelism*, David C Cook, 2011
C. Medearis	*Adventures in Saying 'Yes' – a Journey from fear to faith*, Bethany House, 2015
C. Mallouhi	*Waging Peace on Islam*, Monarch Books, 2002
C. Marsh	*Love Will Find a Way*, OM Books, 1991
C. Marsh	*Share your Faith with a Muslim*, Moody Press, 1980
C. Moucarry	*Faith to Faith – Christianity & Islam in dialogue*, IVP, 2001
R. Scott	*Dear Abdullah – eight questions Muslim people ask about Christianity*, IVP Nottingham 2011
B. Sheikh	*I dared to call him Father*, Kingsway, 2001
V. Stacey	*Meeting Muslims*, OMF Literature, 2006
C. D. Woodberry (Ed)	*From Seed to Fruit*, William Carey Library, 2008
A. Yusuf Ali	*The Holy Qur'an, Text, translation & Commentary*, The Islamic Foundation, 1975
M.A. Qazi	*A Concise Dictionary of Islamic Terms*, Noor Publishing House, 1989

APPENDIX 6

Allah - God of the Bible?

Introduction

It seems that the question "Is 'Allah' the God of the Bible?" is only being asked by western Evangelicals. When I lived for ten years in the Middle East the question never cropped up. Eastern people –Christians and Muslims alike – are puzzled by the question and tend to assume that Judaism, Christianity and Islam are 'Abramic' faiths which means they are historically rooted in Abraham; this makes a Christian and a Muslim 'spiritual cousins'.

To return to the question "Is Allah the God of the Bible?" the answer is both "yes" and "no". There is some evidence on both sides, which is why I believe most westerners come down on one side or the other depending on their heart attitude i.e. Is your focus on the similarities or differences between Islam and Christianity? Is your agenda to construct a bridge for discussion and comparing of spiritual notes (i.e. apologetics) or is your agenda to persuade people to come over to Christian space by discussing the differences (even inadequacies) of Islam? (i.e. polemics)

As a 'grace and truth' response, this resource sets out to explain and unpack the truths of the gospel in the spirit of Jesus, while looking for any evidence, which is in-line with the Bible, as suitable material with which to build the bridge for gospel communication.

The evidence shows that the 'semantic meaning' of the word *Allah* is compatible with God and then leads us to scrutinise the 'spiritual reality' behind the term *Allah*.

Some people tend to think that Muslims have one God and Christians another. While I agree that the two concepts are very different from each other, I cannot agree that they really worship two utterly different gods... my faith in a Christian God was related to my childhood faith in a Muslim God.

When through the book of Psalms and Job I learnt anew the meaning of trust in God, and came to worship Him at the foot of the Cross.

Bishop Teqani Tafti (from Muslim background & former Bishop in Iran)

Linguistic evidence

Linguistically, "*Allah*" is the common Arabic word for one high God. It was used long before Islam began, which is why some of Muhammad's relatives were called things such as "Abdullah" (servant/slave of God). *Allah* is therefore used today by millions of Arabic speaking Christians.

Semantic evidence

Bible translators tell us that over 1,000 different words are used around the world for 'God'. Almost all of them were adopted from existing 'pagan' terms; for example the Greek 'theos', Latin 'deus' and even our English Teutonic word 'God'. The semantics (i.e. 'meaning') of all these were borrowed and refined over time, until they were filled with biblical meaning. Because Muslims use *allah* but don't always appreciate its biblical meaning, is not a sufficient reason to say that Allah is not the God of the Bible.

The Origin of the name of God in the Middle East

El	the ancient high god of the Middle East
Elah (Dan.2:45)	Aramaic word for God (Yahweh)
El-ilah or **Allah**	Arabic word for 'High God'
El-yohn (Gen.14:18-20)	Hebrew word for 'Most High God' (Yahweh)
'alah (the root of El-Elyon)	Hebrew word "to ascend" or "be high"

Historic evidence

The word *allah* comes from the Arabic *el-illah* (the God). For centuries before Abraham, the high god (i.e. *El*) was recognised throughout the Middle East. This is why we find that the Hebrew names for Yahweh mentioned in the Bible, include the prefix El' e.g. E*l-Elyon* (God Most High), *El-Olam* (God of Eternity), *El-Shaddai* (God Almighty). This is why the name Allah did not need introducing when Muhammad recited the Qur'an – it was already known.

However, the reality of its common usage is more messy, because the Arabian desert tribes of Muhammad's time defaulted to popular idolatry, which deified planets; so it's not surprising that *Allah* as the 'high god' became identified with a major planet – the moon and was therefore assumed to be lord of a dynasty of lesser gods; this is called 'henotheism'. In this way *Allah* was said to have three daughters, Al-Lat, Al-Uzza and Menat (S37.149-153; 16.59; 17.41-42). These pagan deities were worshipped along with Satan and *jinn* spirits (S4.116,117; 6.100). The fairytale 'Jinni' of Aladdin's lamp is based on this 'animistic' idea where spirits are deeply respected and manipulated by rituals to gain practical help in daily life.

Remember that God called Abraham when he was part of this sort of pagan culture in Ur of the Chaldeans. This spiritual cocktail also explains Rachel's 'household idols' (Gen.31:30-35) and the presence in Jacob's household of 'foreign gods', alongside the worship of Yahweh (Gen.35:2-4).

Those who say that Allah is not the God and Father of our Lord Jesus Christ are right if they mean that he is not so described by Muslims. They are wrong if they mean that Allah is other than the God of the Christian faith.

Bishop Kenneth Cragg

Hermeneutical evidence

'Talk to the meaning of the other, not merely their words. Refrain from being mere debaters and win the other to your meaning by accessing what lies behind their words. When we hear strident things said by people in pain, we should remember they're hurt. Be patient and reverent with what we don't understand.'

Source: *The Shadow of an Agony*, Oswald Chambers, Discovery House, 1934, pg 17

We need to recognise the reasons behind some Islamic doctrines. The tradition tries to protect the notion of the unity of One God by concluding that the Trinity does not exist and that Jesus is only a Prophet; it also tries to protect Jesus' honour by denying his crucifixion. Many Christians assume Muslims qualify as those who *'deny that Jesus is the Christ? He is anti-Christ who denies the Father and the Son'*. The basic rules of biblical interpretation tell us that the context cannot be referring to Muhammad because it speaks about the past when 'many Antichrists have come' (v18). These were people who were part of the church (i.e. before ever Islam began); and they were Christians who left the church (v19).

Logical evidence

If *Allah* is the God of the Bible in the semantic sense (i.e. meaning) then the next question is whether the spiritual reality behind the name *Allah* is the same as that behind the original 'El' of the Bible. This is the crunch issue.

It's clear that a violent spiritual reality is present within the system of political Islam today. But this is not necessarily evidence that *Allah* is behind this darkness, any more than God is behind the behaviour of the IRA; the brutal Ugandan Lord's Resistance Army; or the actions of violent Christians such as the right wing activist Timothy McVeigh (the Oklahoma bomber).

In Athens Paul referred to a pagan god referred to as the 'Unknown god' (Acts 17:3), not necessarily because of the identity of that god but because what was in the minds of the Greeks was close enough to the true God the Bible is referring to. Paul's assumption is that there can only be one high God under discussion and he judges that there is enough overlap to use the concept as raw material to build the bridge of communication.

The difference between a Muslim and a Christian's perception of God is the difference between an Englishman and a Corsican's perception of the Sun. - i.e. the Englishman sees only clouds and dimmed light and warmth. The Corsican enjoys the full warmth, heat and light. This is a radically different perception of the same reality due to their different vantage points.

Muhammad's evidence

Some scholars argue that what Muhammad began in sincerity and spiritual purity, his close companions politicised after his death. What we do know is that Muhammad was persecuted for preaching righteousness and trying to wean the idol-worshipping Arab tribes away from their gods to the worship of the one God - *Allah* (S38.4). Muhammad himself asserted that Allah is the God of Abraham when he asserted: 'Our God and your God is One; and it is to Him we bow' (S3.84; 29.46).

This helps explain why some Muslims resent the Christian claim that the use of the crescent moon has become the adopted symbol of Islamic religion is because Muslims are idolatrously worshipping the moon. The truth of the matter is that this symbol reflects the fact that the Islamic year, like Judaism, follows a lunar calendar. It is true that a traditional drink to celebrate the end of Ramadan is called *Qamar el-Din* (Moon of religion) but this too is to be expected when it is the new moon Muslims await at the end of the Fast. This sort of anecdotal evidence can be interpreted either way.

People who love, interpret the facts about the one they love more accurately than those who do not love. When our eyes see badly we only notice the darker aspects of what we observe.

John Chrysostom

Pragmatic evidence

The question of whether *Allah* is the God of the Bible is actually a trick question, in the sense that it's like asking: "Have you stopped beating your wife yet?" Without ascertaining if it's true that you used to be guilty of this. You are trapped whatever you say.

The question is therefore best answered by asking some other questions:

1 Is the Muslim idea about God the same as the Christian idea? - No

2 Is there anything in common between the Muslim & Christian ideas of God? - Yes

3 Is there enough in common for us to be able to use the same word? - Yes

On the bases of the above answers we can ask the counter question: "Is the Jesus of the Jehovah's Witnesses the Christ of the Gospels?" The answer has to be "yes" because there is only one Jesus; however the same applies to *Allah* – there is only one God but the Muslim understanding of him is incomplete.

The assumption of Muslim enquirers, and many believers from a Muslim background, gives us confidence that we are in fact talking about the same thing. For example Biquis Sheikh's testimony in her book *'I dared to call Him Father'* is an example of 'continuity' rather than 'discontinuity'. Biquis said that through Christ, she had found the God she had worshipped from a respectable distance, all her life. She found the completion of her Islam in Christ – some elements were dispensed with as incompatible with the Bible while other elements were affirmed by the Bible.

Friendship First therefore takes the pragmatic view that if Allah is not the God of the Bible, it blows Muslims and Christians totally apart as alien traditions (i.e. on a par with Hinduism) rather than mono-theistic first cousins. The challenge of meaningful discussion would become almost impossible for many and the situation intolerable for others.

Islam presents an inadequate and incomplete – but not totally misguided - view of God. It seems unfair to say that the God of Islam is absolutely distinct from the God of the Bible

Phil Parshall

Conclusion

This is why it's a more strategic starting point to see *Allah* as the God of the Bible, with the proviso that the Muslim understanding of him is what needs to change. If there is darkness within the Islamic system, it does not give us permission to conclude that *Allah* is a demonic entity – something that is as confusing for Arabic-speaking Christians and Muslims as it is offensive. Patient discussion based on the actual text of Bible and Qur'an, is the only way.

The stunning revelation for Muslims and Christians alike is the truth Jesus is *Emmanu-El* i.e. the "High God" of the universe who is now "with us". Jesus is Lord of all life and by God's grace many more Muslims will yet come to know this.

www.ingramcontent.com/pod-product-compliance
Lightning Source LLC
Chambersburg PA
CBHW060801100426
42813CB00004B/903

* 9 7 8 0 9 9 5 7 7 8 7 7 1 *